PSALMS 1–72

EPWORTH PREACHER'S COMMENTARIES

*

PSALMS 1-72

*

CYRIL S. RODD
M.A.

EPWORTH PRESS

LONDON : THE EPWORTH PRESS

FIRST PUBLISHED IN 1963

© THE EPWORTH PRESS 1963

Book Steward
FRANK H. CUMBERS

SET IN MONOTYPE TIMES ROMAN AND PRINTED IN
GREAT BRITAIN BY THE CAMELOT PRESS LTD
LONDON AND SOUTHAMPTON

General Introduction

WE are living in a day in which the authority and message of the Bible is being rediscovered and declared. Preachers are realizing afresh that their message must be based on the Word of God in Scripture. Many commentaries on the books of the Bible are already available, and give much space to the consideration of critical questions and historical and literary problems.

This new series of commentaries, as its name suggests, is written specifically for preachers, and particularly for those who feel themselves ill-equipped to study the more advanced works of scholarship. Its aim is to set forth the essential message of the Bible. Questions of authorship, date, background, will be dealt with briefly, and only in so far as they are necessary for informed preaching. The main purpose of each commentary will be (*a*) to explain the original meaning of each biblical passage, and (*b*) to indicate its relevance to human need in the present situation. Bearing in mind this dual purpose, each author will have freedom to use what method of treatment he thinks most suitable to the book of the Bible on which he is commenting.

To save space, the biblical text is not printed, but the commentary is based on that of the *Revised Version*.

This, the eleventh volume of the Epworth Preacher's Commentaries, is the first of two volumes on the Psalms. That on Ps 73–150 will be published in six months' time. The author is the Rev. Cyril S. Rodd who, after a few years in circuit work, was called in 1956 to the Chair of Old Testament Language and Literature at Handsworth College, Birmingham.

Mr Rodd does not attempt to give an exact dating to the individual psalms, but suggests 'the broad periods to which they belong'. He closely links the Psalter with the temple cultus, but recognizes that some scholars take a different point of view. His special Note on 'the imprecatory psalms' sheds much light on a familiar and difficult problem.

This Commentary will surely achieve the author's purpose, and kindle in many a preacher 'a desire to take a psalm and preach Christ'.   GREVILLE P. LEWIS

Three Notes by way of Preface

1. ALL that is of value in the present commentary is stolen from others. The lack of acknowledgement in footnotes is not a sign of ingratitude.

2. The divine name is reproduced as Yahweh, in accordance with the general policy of the series. The present writer, however, is of the firm opinion that 'Yahweh' should never be used in sermons or any part of Church worship. His own practice is to use 'the Lord' or 'Jehovah', names which give a greater sense of worship and have a more ancient tradition behind them.

3. This makes no pretence at being a critical commentary. Scholars will find nothing in it to waste their midnight hours in reading. Students will discover nothing to transfer to the pages of examination answers. A Methodist preacher has simply tried to show how he would preach on the psalms. His efforts will not tell other preachers all they want to know, but it is hoped that they will stir the imagination and kindle a desire to take a psalm and preach Christ.

Abbreviations

AV, RV	Authorized and Revised Versions
*RV*m	Revised Version marginal reading
RSV	*Revised Standard Version*
AT	*The Bible, An American Translation* (edit. J. M. Powis Smith and Edgar J. Goodspeed. Chicago, 1939)
M	*Moffatt* (Hodder and Stoughton, 1935)
NEB	*New English Bible* (NT, Oxford and Cambridge, 1961)
PBV	Prayer Book Version
MHB	*Methodist Hymn-book* (1933)

Introduction

The Approach

MODERN hymn-books usually arrange the hymns according to their subjects, rather than lumping them together as 'general hymns', or collecting them by authors as in many anthologies of poetry. This helps both those who select hymns for services and those who use the hymn book in private devotions. The Psalter, however, has no such consistent arrangement, largely because it was compiled from a number of smaller collections.

The older approach, which treated all the psalms separately, was suggested by the titles attached to many of them. According to temperament, the more conservative assumed that the ascription 'of David' meant that he was the author and attempted to defend the titles, assigning the psalms to specific incidents in his life, while the more radical rejected the evidence of the titles and ranged freely over the whole of Israelite history down to Maccabaean times, in their efforts to find a historical setting suitable to each psalm. These attempts failed because the supposed historical allusions in the psalms are far too general to support exact dating. The most that can be done is to suggest the broad periods to which they belong.

A more fruitful line was opened up by the realization that, in the ancient world, the structure of different types of hymns was relatively fixed, the correct form of words being almost as important as the correct ordering of sacrificial ritual. On this basis it is possible to classify a majority of the psalms, and six main groups may be noticed.

(i) *Hymns of Praise*. These normally consist of a call to praise Yahweh, followed by a statement of the reasons for worshipping Him. They can be seen in **29, 100, 145–150**.

(ii) *Laments of the Community*. When famine or defeat in battle threatened the nation, a fast would be called and the people would express their grief and call upon Yahweh for help (see 1 Kings 8^{33-6}). Such a plea would be expressed in a psalm, and there are examples in **44, 74, 79**, and **80**.

(iii) *Laments of an Individual*. These form the largest class.

The worshipper is in distress and calls on God for deliverance. Usually the suffering is described in very general terms; often sickness (**22, 38, 88**) or the attacks of enemies (**3, 5, 17, 109**) are mentioned.

(iv) *Thanksgiving of an Individual.* When a man received the answer to his prayer and was delivered from his distress, he would offer thanksgiving to God with a psalm. Often these psalms contain an account of the distress from which God has saved him. Examples are **30, 32, 34, 66, 116.**

(v) *Royal Psalms.* These are psalms which have the king as the central figure, and it may be assumed that they come from the period before the exile (see **2, 45, 72**). Although the group contains different types of psalms, it is useful to place them together, since this draws attention to the important place the king had in the life of the nation.

(vi) *Wisdom Poetry.* The writings of the wise men were current throughout the ancient world and are found in the wisdom books of the OT—*Proverbs, Job* and *Ecclesiastes.* Some of this wisdom poetry is also included in the Psalter. There are two kinds: collections of proverbs loosely strung together (see **127**), and poems in which some theme is developed (as in **1, 49, 73**).

The advantage of such a classification is that it is derived from the psalms themselves and is not imposed upon them, as any arbitrary arrangement by subjects would be. It has, moreover, led to a richer understanding of the use of the psalms in Israelite worship.

The Place of the Psalms in Israelite Worship

It seems highly probable that most of the psalms were used in the worship of the temple or other sanctuaries. Even the songs of the individual were probably composed by officials of the sanctuary for the use of worshippers who came to plead their cause with God or to express their thanksgiving. This would explain the lack of personal allusions and the references to paying vows (22^{22-5}, 54^6, 56^{12}), and to the presence of other worshippers (66^{13-20}, 116^{13-19}). The striking change of tone in some of the psalms, from desperate pleading to joyous certainty that God has heard the prayer, may have come in response to some 'sign' or a word from a prophet (see 6^{8-10}, 140^{12-13}). Some of the individual laments may have been the prayers of those seeking the vindication of their innocence (see **4, 7**).

The Royal Psalms and a group of Hymns which celebrate Yahweh as King (the 'Enthronement Psalms', **47, 93, 95-9**) may have been sung in the feast of Ingathering, the chief pre-exilic festival (Ex 23^{16}, Lev 23$^{33-6}$). It has been plausibly suggested that Yahweh was worshipped as the Lord of nature who secured for His people the autumn rains on which their prosperity depended (see **29, 93**), and as the Lord of morality to whom the people renewed their vows of obedience (see **24, 95**). There was probably a ritual drama, in which the ark, representing Yahweh's presence, was carried in procession, and Yahweh was portrayed overcoming His enemies and bringing in a universal reign of righteousness and peace (**24, 46, 82, 98**). The king seems to have taken a prominent part in this ritual. As the representative of the people, he was attacked by his nation's foes and almost defeated, when, at the moment of his deepest distress, Yahweh intervened and saved him, finally enthroning him as His adopted son and giving him a world dominion (see **2, 18, 89, 101, 118**).

It is only fair to add that this interpretation is not accepted by all scholars. Some see the Royal Psalms as belonging to actual events in the life of the king, rather than to a cultic ritual, and view the Enthronement Psalms as hymns based on the prophecies of Second Isaiah. The space available in this commentary has meant that little further discussion of these highly controversial matters is possible, and the cultic view has been adopted as seeming to the present writer to explain more features of the psalms than any other.

The Psalms in Christian Worship

The psalms belong to the time before the coming of Christ, and although the Christian believes that the same God was active in the Old Testament as in the New, he recognizes that many passages express ideas which fall short of the Christian faith and some are even contrary to it. To refuse to go beyond the meaning which the psalm had for those who first sang it would seriously impoverish our spiritual life, however, for the Christian always fills out the revelation which came to Israel with his own understanding of God in Jesus Christ. Even such a passage as Isaiah 53 is probably far richer for him than it was for the prophet himself. In devotion and in preaching we must pass easily across into the NT faith.

Difficulty arises, nevertheless, where there is no natural development of ideas. Some passages cannot be reconciled to the Christian revelation. The only course open here is to say, 'We have not so learned Christ'. To use these passages in Christian worship may mislead the immature and give a false picture of the faith. They can scarcely be justified by any attempt at 'spiritualizing' the ideas, though hard sayings should not be lightly discarded by an emasculated faith.

Other psalms belong to situations and a world of ideas so different from ours that Christian interpretation tends not merely to go beyond the original meaning but to bring in ideas which the original writer never intended. There is no need to go far into the fantasies of allegory to see this. Charles Wesley's paraphrases on **45** and Deuteronomy 33[26–9] (*MHB* 270 and 68) provide illustrations, and there are NT precedents (e.g. Heb 2[6–8]). Personal prejudice largely determines one's attitude to this. Familiar and beautiful words have always been retained and reinterpreted in the life of religion, and, although the humanist may stigmatize this as a dishonest 'double-think', there seems to be little danger, so long as one recognizes what is being done and neither believes that anything has been 'proved' by this nor that this was after all the 'real' meaning of the passage.

Books for further reading

Commentaries

A. B. Rhodes, *Psalms* (S.C.M. Layman's Bible Commentaries). This is an excellent, straightforward exposition.

E. A. Leslie, *The Psalms* (Abingdon Press). The psalms are set in the life and worship of Israel, and a new translation is given, but from an emended text.

A. F. Kirkpatrick, *The Book of Psalms* (Cambridge Bible). Although out of date in some ways, the comments always show spiritual perception and sound scholarship.

A. Weiser, *The Psalms* (S.C.M.). A full length commentary, translated from the original German.

Other Books

A. R. Johnson, *Sacral Kingship* (University of Wales Press). A detailed study of the psalms connected with the New Year

Festival at Jerusalem, to which the present writer is very greatly indebted.

G. S. Gunn, *God in the Psalms* (Saint Andrew Press). A study of the theology of the psalms.

A Note on Modern Translations

In line with other commentaries in this series, this commentary is based on the *RV*. This keeps closely to the Hebrew text, but it does not deal radically enough with some difficulties and its literalism can give a distorted picture of Hebrew piety.

The *RSV* often gives a better translation and is generally to be preferred. Particularly to be noted are the more precise translations of psychological terms; thus 'soul' never means the immortal spirit which has been imprisoned within the body, but is the equivalent of 'life' or 'person', and 'my soul' often means 'I myself', while 'heart' is more often the centre of the thought or the will rather than of the emotions.

Moffatt gives a vigorous rendering, but is rather too ready to emend.

The little known 'American Translation' was the work of a group of scholars, the psalms being translated by J. M. Powis Smith. It takes into account work which had been done on the psalms up to that time, but unfortunately changes which have been made in the text are not noted.

Where there is no note after renderings which differ from the *RV* in the present commentary, I have ventured to make my own translation or paraphrase.

Commentary

1. Ah, the Happiness of the Righteous

A wisdom writer sets out his ideal of the good man and the blessing which comes to him.

1¹. '*scornful*'. The proud and self-confident men who scoff at all that is sacred and good (see Prov 13¹, 15¹², 21²⁴).

1⁵. '*shall not stand in the judgement*'. Probably not the last judgement. The psalmist believes God will remove the wicked from the daily life of Israel and her religious assemblies.

1⁶. '*knoweth*'. God's knowledge of us is never that of an impartial social observer. He watches over us with loving care (see Deut 2⁷), and since He desires our true welfare He punishes our sin (see Amos 3²).

The psalm begins with a beatitude: Ah, the happiness of the man who keeps aloof from evil men and sets his mind on God. To notice this is to avoid the mistaken idea that the writer is a legalist, interested in retribution alone. It is true that he presents the contrast between the wicked and the good, and points to the 'two ways', but his eye is fixed on the righteous. Only the godly man is described in detail; the side glance at the wicked is but to light up the blessing of his life by contrast. Like Jesus in Matthew 5, the psalmist is confident that the good life is attractive and brings real happiness, not any cloistered 'blessedness'. This needs to be reasserted in every age. 'The pleasures of sin' are real pleasures and can entice because they appear very desirable. Over against them must be set the full attractiveness of the good life.

Yet how difficult it is to depict goodness. We all know evil at first hand, but we cannot even imagine what it is like to be entirely good. Even Milton made Satan more interesting than God. The psalmist picks out two features of the life of the good man: he avoids all evil persons and he delights in God's law. The law to him is no heavy yoke, but the gift of God's grace, joyously to be received and obeyed. In it God has revealed His love and has given teaching which enables men to live the good life, to serve Him and to attain lasting happiness in fellowship with Himself. He reads it over to himself half aloud until it has become part of the very fibre of his being. (On the 'Law' see **119** and the notes there.)

The Christian will feel that simply to separate himself from evil-doers in order to remain unspotted from the world is to fall below the way of Christ, for He was called the 'friend of publicans and sinners' (Mt 11¹⁹, cf. Mk 2¹⁵⁻¹⁷). Yet even of Jesus it was said that He was 'separated from sinners' (Heb 7²⁶). There is no contradiction here. He was both true friend of sinners and so separated from them that not even His bitterest enemies accused Him of being tainted by their vices. The timid aloofness of the psalmist is not for us; we need the spiritual strength which takes the risk of standing by the side of the bad man as a real friend, and can bear the cost.

While the main emphasis of the psalm is on the call to the good life, the psalmist cannot overlook its consequences. He uses familiar pictures of prosperity and destruction—the tree planted beside the irrigation canals (cf. Jer 17⁸, Ezek 47¹²), and the chaff blown away by the wind when the corn was winnowed on the hill tops of Palestine (cf. Hos 13³). If such exact retribution does not always follow, and sickness comes to the best of men, at least it is broadly true that honesty and integrity find their reward even in this life, and the upright life does lead to our highest good. It is left to other psalms (see **49** and **73**) and to the book of *Job* to consider the problem more deeply. To the writer of the present psalm, this reward is no automatic working of an impersonal law, but the loving care of God who '*knoweth the way of the righteous*'.

The psalmist is certain of the happiness of the good man. An even greater beatitude is found in **32**¹: 'Ah, the happiness of the man whose rebellion against God is forgiven'.

2. The Enthronement of the Lord's Anointed

This psalm belongs to the religious drama of the temple and seems to come towards the end of that ritual. The king has been saved from his enemies by the power of God and now he proclaims his position as the adopted son of God, supreme over all his foes.

2². '*anointed*'. Messiah—but here the king of Israel is intended. This is not a messianic prophecy.

2⁹. '*Thou shalt break them with a rod of iron*'. The Greek version reads with different vowels, 'shepherd, rule, them', and this is the text of the psalm used in Rev 2²⁷, 12⁵, 19¹⁵.

2¹¹⁻¹². The *RV* translation is very doubtful. It is better to read as *RSV*, slightly altering the text,

> 'Serve the LORD with fear,
> with trembling kiss his feet' (as an act of homage).

The scenes in the drama are finely drawn. The psalm opens in a tone of astonished wonder that the foreign kings should have plotted to rebel against Yahweh and His anointed king. Such plots were usual in the great empires of the ancient East on the death of the king, when all the vassal states rose in revolt. The writer may have based his psalm on hymns sung in Babylon. This would explain the extravagant language, for not even David's kingdom was a world empire. Some have thought that the psalm was sung at the enthronement of a king, and David, Solomon and other kings have been suggested. It is more probable that it belongs to an annual ritual at Jerusalem at which a group of the psalms were sung (see e.g. **21, 24, 46, 48, 72, 82, 93, 95, 97, 99, 101, 110, 132**). Many important religious ideas were expressed in this ritual. Here the dominant theme is the sovereignty of God and of the king, His anointed (verses 1–3).

Moving to the heavenly court, we hear God's mocking laughter. He is in control of the whole world and rebellion is futile. The poet boldly uses human terms of God, and some feel that he sinks below the spiritual levels of other psalms. But God is personal even if He is more than merely a man enlarged, and the most spiritual religion must have a vivid consciousness of the living and active God. This is not to say, however, that the God who holds His enemies in derision is fully the Christian God (verses 4–6).

The king now speaks. He recalls the word of God given to

B

him when he first became king. He is heir to the promise in
2 Samuel 7[14]. He is God's adopted son and hence ruler of all
the kingdoms of the world as God's representative. In the
ancient world many kings regarded themselves as sons of
God. The Israelite king was always clearly a man and no
demigod, though his specially close relationship to God could
be described as adopted sonship (verses 7–9).

The final section of the psalm returns to the earthly rulers
who are urged to submit to God, for while His anger is terrible
there is blessing in taking refuge in Him (verses 10–12).

The NT writers looked upon this psalm as messianic
prophecy pointing to Jesus (see Acts 4[25-8], 13[33], Heb 1[5], 5[5]).
The psalmist was thinking of the earthly king in Israel and
not of a future messiah, but it was natural to see a fulfilment
in Christ. To us a king who breaks the nations with a rod of
iron and dashes them in pieces like an earthenware jar is very
different from the crucified Jesus who prayed forgiveness for
His enemies. But Jesus is no less a victorious king because
His triumph was the conquest of love. He won his victories
by offering friendship to notorious sinners, going into their
homes, eating and drinking with them, and making them now
desire goodness (see Lk 19[1-10]). His victory was won on the
Cross where He refused to allow the cruelty and evil of men to
defeat His love no less than at the resurrection. And those
who now pay the true homage of loving gratitude are those
who have been found in His loving search for the lost, and
have themselves discovered the beatitude with which the
psalm ends: 'Ah, the happiness of those who seek refuge in
God,' God who is enthroned in the heavens and who raised
Jesus from the dead (see Lk 7[36-50]).

> *Extol His kingly power,*
> *Kiss the exalted Son,*
> *Who died; and lives, to die no more,*
> *High on His Father's throne;*
> *Our Advocate with God,*
> *He undertakes our cause,*
> *And spreads through all the earth abroad*
> *The victory of His Cross.* (*MHB* 243)

It is little wonder that this psalm has been traditionally
associated with Easter Day in the Church.

3. Confidence in God in the midst of Enemies

This individual lament is marked by a deep trust in God.

3². '*my soul*'. Soul in Hebrew thought is not the complement of the body, but is roughly the equivalent of our 'person' (see Gen 2⁷, 'and man became a *living being*', *RSV*). Here the phrase means 'me' as *RSV*.

'*Selah*'. The meaning of this word is doubtful. It may indicate an instrumental interlude between the strophes of a psalm.

3³. The section expressing the psalmist's trust does not begin with 'I' but with 'Thou'. Trust is grounded in God, not in the strength of our faith.

The psalmist prays to God for deliverance from his adversaries. He does not say who these enemies are. The title suggests they were David's rebellious subjects at the time of Absalom's revolt, but the titles of the psalms can be regarded as no more than the earliest attempts to set them in historical situations. Sometimes in these individual laments the enemies seem to be those who see the psalmists' sicknesses as a proof that they have committed great sins; instead of offering comfort they point an accusing finger (see 6). At other times it may be that the psalm was recited when a man was brought before the priests on a criminal charge and his enemies are those who accuse him (see 4, 7, and Deut 17⁸⁻¹³). Possibly some of these laments were originally written for the king when he was facing foreign enemies, or took part in a ritual combat in the temple festivals, and they have now been taken over by ordinary Israelites for use in time of trouble (see verse 6).

The writer's enemies say that he will find little help in his God, but he is full of confidence. He knows God from personal experience as One who answers his prayers. So confident is he that he can lie down and sleep, not kept awake by any anxious fears; a sure test of the depth of his faith. Now he again makes his appeal to God to save him, an appeal based on that earlier trust.

Frequently towards the end of individual laments there is a striking change of tone such as is found in verse 7b (cf. 4⁷⁻⁸,

6^{8-10}). Using what must have been no more than metaphors
to him, he tells how God *has* saved him by crushing his foes.
Often this change to certainty seems to be the result of some
word of God or sign which is given to the psalmist in the
temple, though in this psalm the final section may be his thanksgiving after his deliverance.

The final verse is a confession of faith and a blessing on the
community. To those who have experienced God's salvation,
a creed is no bare form of words. We truly say 'Jesus is
Lord' when we know Him as Lord of our life (see Rom 10^9).

4. The Joy of one Vindicated by God

Justice was usually administered by the elders as they sat in
the gate of the city (see Ruth 4^{1-2}, Amos $5^{10, 12, 15}$). Difficult cases, however, might be decided by God Himself through
a ritual in the sanctuary as regulated in Exodus 22^{7-9} and
Deuteronomy 17^{8-13} (cf. 1 Kings 8^{31-2}). This psalm seems to be
the prayer of one who has received such a decision in his
favour and yet has still to face accusations from influential
enemies.

4^3. Perhaps we should translate, with a slight change of text,
'Know that Yahweh has shown His wonderful love to me'.

4^5. '*sacrifices of righteousness*'. Not offering righteousness
as a substitute for sacrifice, but sacrifices offered with the
correct ritual or those which are rightly required.

4^6. The second line is a reminiscence of the priestly blessing in Numbers 6^{24-6}, but it seems a little out of place
here. Perhaps read, 'The light of Thy presence has departed
from us'.

The psalmist first offers his prayer to the '*God of my righteousness*'—God who has vindicated him and released him from a
narrow, frustrating life into the broad freedom of salvation.
He then turns to his accusers. Why do they persist in their
false accusations and their plans to subvert this judgement?
God has shown His wonderful love to him, probably through
some concrete word or sign in the temple, and He will continue to protect him and answer his prayers. He urges them

to cease from these sinful designs and to restrain their evil thoughts. Let them find peace of mind by trustfully sacrificing to God.

In verses 6–8 the psalmist contrasts the fretful grumbling of those who do not trust in God with his own joy and peace. They can see nothing good in life and do not even recognize God when He is near at hand. He has joy greater than that of peasants at a time of bountiful harvest, and a confidence in God which gives him sleep free from all restless wakefulness even when he is utterly alone.

The joy and peace seen in this psalm are the fruit of the Spirit for the Christian (Gal 5²²). Jesus gives His peace to those who have known God's salvation (see Mk 5³⁴, Lk 7⁵⁰, Jn 14²⁷, 16³³, Rom 5¹, Phil 4⁷).

5. 'In the multitude of thy lovingkindness'

One falsely accused makes his morning prayer to God.

5³. '*will I order* my prayer *unto thee*'. As *RV* italics show, no object is expressed in the original. It may be that the object should be 'my sacrifice' as in *RSV* (cf. Lev 1⁷, ⁸). Sacrifice (and sacrament) need be no bare external formality to the spiritual man, but can be an aid to his approach to God.

5⁴. '*Evil shall not sojourn with thee*'. Perhaps 'the evil man', who cannot be God's guest, enjoying the privileges of His hospitality. It is just possible that the meaning is, 'Evil does not attract Thee', as it does men. Really to desire goodness and not to be attracted by evil mark the saint who is perfect as his heavenly Father is perfect.

At first sight many of the psalms are tediously alike. In individual laments, the psalmists frequently appeal to God against enemies and assert their own righteousness over against these 'workers of iniquity'. This is to be expected, however, if the psalms belong to cultic rituals and have a particular style from their place in that ritual. Indeed, it is just this similarity which makes more satisfactory the approach accepted by most scholars today and adopted in this commentary, which does not attempt to interpret the psalms as isolated poems, but tries to understand them in their setting in the life and worship of Israel. Yet this similarity is no dull uniformity. Each psalm has some special emphasis or characteristic.

The present individual lament seems to have been used by the falsely accused as he offers a sacrifice in the temple and awaits God's sign of his acquittal. Towards his enemies he has a hostility which seems far from Christian love. But two facts need to be remembered: (1) the psalm has a cultic setting and the ritual will contrast the plaintiff and his accusers as forcibly as a modern law court; (2) the writer makes no distinction between the evil man and his sin as we often claim to do. The wicked man is a rebel against God and must face God's condemnation.

The confident trust in God in this psalm is its distinctive characteristic. The psalmist prays to God in His transcendent glory as King, yet he knows He is One who can be approached by the humblest individual, for He is '*my King, and my God*' (verse 2). He knows, moreover, that he can come into the house of God only because of God's great mercy and love (verse 7). As Christians, we miss the wonder of our faith if we are so absorbed in a God who is a loving Father that we forget He is also God, exalted in transcendent majesty, who can be worshipped by man only because He has stooped down to be our Friend, and approached only because we can come trusting in His grace in Jesus Christ.

Trust and worship lead to action. Because God does not delight in wickedness and cannot be addressed by those who do evil, the psalmist desires to know God's way and to be led in this life by Him who is not merely just, but also the faithful Protector of those who trust in Him (see **25** for this 'way' of God).

Those who come to God as this psalmist did can do no other but rejoice (verses 11–12).

6. The Prayer of a Sick Man

In this psalm a sick man prays to God in the sanctuary and receives the assurance that his prayer is heard.

6⁷. '*wasteth away*'. The word probably means, 'grows dim, dark or dull'.

'*mine adversaries*'. Possibly 'the hostility towards me'.

The psalmist is ill and, weakened perhaps by some fever, he despairs of life. His suffering is increased by his belief that his illness comes directly from an angry God as punishment for sin. How often, even today, the sufferer believes this and cries out, 'What have I done to deserve this? Why does God let this happen to me?'

His suffering is increased yet more as he faces the prospect of death, for he has no hope of any real future life. There is only Sheol, a dark underworld where the dead live out a shadowy existence, remembering nothing of their past life or God's goodness to them, having no opportunity to praise Him, and standing beyond the reach of His love. Even the greatest king becomes weak as he descends into the land of shades and dust and silence (see **30⁹, 88¹⁰⁻¹², 115¹⁷**, Isa 14⁹⁻¹⁵). The psalmist lives before Christ came, and has to face his suffering without Him who shared flesh and blood 'that he might deliver all them who through fear of death were all their lifetime subject to bondage' (Heb 2¹⁴⁻¹⁵).

His suffering is made more intense by those about him. They too believe that illness is God's punishment for sin. Hence they offer no sympathy or help but only throw accusations at one whom God now condemns, in the same way that Job's friends, while they came to console him, end by accusing him of some hidden sin which deserves an even heavier penalty (see Job 11⁶, 15⁴⁻⁶, 22⁵⁻¹¹). This is a more probable interpretation of the '*workers of iniquity*' in verse 8 than that they are the personal enemies of the psalmist, or members of a rival party, or even sorcerers who have brought the illness upon him. How difficult it is to give real sympathy when we understand others so little—how much more difficult if we have a false belief about God.

The psalmist appeals to God out of the midst of this suffering. He prays first of all on the ground of the suffering. '*How long?*' The two words tell more than all his descriptions of his sufferings and the tears which drain the lustre from his eyes. How long will God be estranged from him and withdraw His favour? How long will he have to endure? This is the measure of suffering—the weary struggle to bear the pain and weakness, the dark future which lies ahead unknown. But the heart of his prayer is in verse 4, '*Save me for thy lovingkindness' sake*'. There is no confession in the psalm, although it is counted the first of the Penitential Psalms of the ancient Church and

associated with Ash Wednesday, and some find it strange that
a man who sees his suffering as punishment should not confess
his sin. Perhaps this fails to understand how suffering can
crush a man. The psalmist, however, reaches out beyond
penitence. He turns away from himself, his sorrows, pains,
fears, and even sins, to God and God's love shown to His
people, confirmed in His covenant, enduring as His glorious
majesty itself, and, the Christian would add, proved to us 'in
that, while we were yet sinners, Christ died for us' (Rom 5⁸).

The change of tone in verses 8–10 is so striking that some
have thought that they form a separate psalm, perhaps the
thanksgiving after recovery. Others have spoken of a sudden
inspiration of faith which gives the psalmist an inward assurance that God has heard his prayer and will answer it. It
seems more likely that this psalm was recited by a sufferer in
the temple, and that between verses 7 and 8 a priest or prophet
carried out an atonement ritual or gave a word from God, or
even that the recital of Yahweh's gracious dealings with
Israel gave him the certainty that this God had heard his
prayer and would confound his enemies.

A psalm which speaks of the wrath of God causing sickness,
and which has a meagre hope beyond the grave and no love
of enemies, may seem to have little for the Christian. The
contrast with life in Christ might be emphasized, but it is wiser
to fasten on verse 4, 'for the sake of Thy constant love'.

7. The Accused takes an Oath of Innocence

In his prayer at the dedication of the temple Solomon prays,
'If a man sins against his neighbour and is made to take an
oath, and comes and swears his oath before thine altar in this
house, then hear thou in heaven, and act, and judge thy servants, condemning the guilty by bringing his conduct upon his
own head, and vindicating the righteous by rewarding him
according to his righteousness' (1 Kings 8³¹⁻³², *RSV*; see also
Ex 22¹¹). This psalm is probably a form of words used in this
ceremony.

7². '*my soul*'. Probably here the word means 'throat' as in
Jonah 2⁵. Those who accuse the psalmist are compared to a
lion which seizes his throat and mauls him, while no-one steps
forward to help. He must rely on God alone, a sure Deliverer.

7⁴ᵇ. Difficult. *RV* regards this as an expression of the psalmist's superlative goodness, but there is no hint of such a contrast with the first part of the verse in the original. *RSV*, taking the verb in a rather improbable sense, translates: 'or plundered my enemy without cause'. Perhaps the meaning is, 'or allowed my enemy to escape without cause', an unchristian sentiment, but one found elsewhere in the psalms.

7⁷. '*return thou*'. Probably read 'take thy seat' as a judge, as in *RSV*.

7¹²ᵃ. *RSV* makes explicit the meaning of *RV:*

'If a man does not repent,
God will whet his sword.'

Probably, however, the whole verse describes the actions of the wicked man, and the line should be translated, 'Again, indeed, he sharpens his sword' (cf. *RV*m).

After a short introductory prayer, the man who has been accused utters his oath of clearance (verses 3–5). It may be compared with Job's great oath in Job 31, where he declares his innocence from many sins and reveals an ethic which is worthy to be set alongside that of the NT. Here the psalmist protests that he has not wronged his friend, and he will be referring to some specific crime. Like Job he invokes a curse upon himself should he be guilty, and later in the psalm he appeals to God to vindicate him since he is innocent (verse 8). Such assertions of 'righteousness' and personal goodness are found in other psalms and appear to us arrogant and pharisaical. Some of these psalms tell of the king's deliverance by God because of his faithful dependence on Him, and in these righteousness has a special significance (see on **18** and **101**). Here and in **26** the setting of the psalm shows that 'righteousness' means little more than that the accused is innocent of the particular charge. (For a discussion of apparently self-righteous claims to goodness see on **17**.)

Verses 6–11 depict Yahweh sitting in judgement. He is judge of all the nations, a conception probably derived from the annual temple festival in Jerusalem in which Yahweh establishes His justice over all the earth after He has saved His anointed king (see **82** and **98**). The longing that God will

defeat evil and bring in His kingdom of righteousness finds
its fulfilment in Christ, who won the victory over sin on the
Cross and now gives His righteousness to those who live by
faith in Him. In this psalm, however, the dominant thought
is that God is the just judge who condemns the guilty and
acquits the innocent. The desire for such justice was wide-
spread in the east where corruption was common (see Ex 23[6-7],
Deut 25[1], Prov 17[15] and the condemnations of the prophets in
Isa 1[23], 5[23], 10[2], 29[21], Amos 5[12]). How great a blessing is
impartial and certain justice (see **72**). Paul, nevertheless,
speaks of God acquitting the guilty (Rom 3[23-4], 4[5]), exactly
what the *unjust* judges did, and modern theologians glory in
the 'sheer paradox' of this. Yet is it satisfactory to have
to set in such stark opposition the justice which confers so
great benefits on society and the justification which is claimed
to be central to the Christian faith? Paul's paradox, in
fact, shows that you cannot speak of God's dealings with
sinful men in terms of a law court at all. To do this is to
arrive at blank contradiction. You need the language of the
home.

The general sense of verses 12–16 is plain—the evil which
men do will recoil upon their own heads. This is a common
idea in the OT where the result of sin (punishment) is regarded
as being intimately linked to the evil action. Indeed, Exodus
23[33] and Deuteronomy 7[16] may describe idolatry as a 'boom-
erang' which returns with its punishment upon the people who
serve other gods. If retribution is not quite as automatic as
this, evil does have its consequences. Burns wrote of the
dreadful hardening which followed his amours. To commit
sin weakens the desire and appreciation of goodness as well as
making it harder to do right.

The psalmist concludes with thankful praise to the Almighty
God, who has shown His willingness to help an individual
Israelite who had left the proof of his innocence in His keeping.
This is how God reveals His 'righteousness'.

8. God the Creator

This is a hymn of praise to God, the majestic Lord of the
universe, who adds to the wonders of His natural creation the
wonders of His grace by remembering and caring for man and
giving him authority over His world.

8¹. '*Who hast set thy glory upon the heavens*'. As *RV*m shows, this is the reading of some of the ancient translations. It may be that the Hebrew intends, 'Whose majesty is sung above the heavens' (cf. *RSV*).

8². '*hast thou established strength*'. Rather, 'Thou hast founded a stronghold' (cf. *RSV*). Some would read, 'Thou hast admonished the mighty,' though this is less striking. The former translation means that God is so mighty that the praises of children are a sufficient fortress against His enemies. Among these enemies the psalmist may include the hostile forces of chaos who had to be quelled before the ordered world was created.

8⁵. '*God*'. The Greek version translates by 'the angels'. It is possible that the psalmist was thinking of those divine members of the heavenly court who attend on God (see **82, 103²¹,** 1 Kings 22¹⁹), though even these are more exalted than our angels; but it is more likely that the verse asserts that man is but little lower than God Himself (cf. Gen 1²⁶⁻⁷).

The whole congregation lifts up its voice to God in adoration: 'O Yahweh, our Lord, how majestic is Thy name in all the earth.' The splendour of Israel's God is praised in earth and heaven. True worship begins when men have this vivid sense of the transcendent glory of God.

In verse 3 a soloist takes up the main theme. Gazing at the full-starred heavens he quickly passes from their beauty to their Maker. These heavens are the work of God's fingers. The finger of God is mentioned only on four occasions in the Bible and each is important. The Egyptian magicians declare that the plagues which led to the Exodus deliverance are brought by the finger of God (Ex 8¹⁹). God wrote the law of the Sinai covenant with His finger (Ex 31¹⁸, Deut 9¹⁰). Jesus declares that His miracles are performed through the finger of God, miracles which show that God's kingdom has come to men (Lk 11²⁰). Creation, Exodus, Law-giving, Incarnation— the points of decisive action in God's dealings with men.

Over against God and the immensity of His created heavens the psalmist sets man. Small and frail as he is, God has bestowed on him His special love and care. It is not that the psalmist is setting out the natural dignity of man and his inalienable and sacred rights. Man may seem to be the summit of creation, yet it is God who crowned him with glory and honour. He may be able to control the whole of nature but this authority comes from God.

What is man? Scientific discovery has cut man down to size and made him more insignificant than the psalmist ever imagined. In a universe of immense empty spaces the inhabitants of one small planet attached to a mediocre star seem to have no value at all. The pessimistic hypothesis would see man as emerging in a blind world-process, utterly alone in the vast deserts of a universe which is neither friendly nor unfriendly, for there is no Intelligence behind or within it. As a race man exists for a mere million years, as an individual for less than one hundred. Any goodness which he may achieve is transient and when mankind ceases to exist there is no-one to lament its passing, for although other equally shortlived races of beings possessing mind and conscience may arise in other distant parts of the universe, they will know nothing of the achievements of men on this earth. The most that the unbeliever can say to this is that it is hateful, for to say that it is absurd is to assume that there is at least a Mind behind the universe. To faith, however, astronomy only intensifies the marvel of God's grace. Men may be no more than maggots crawling on the surface of this earth, but 'He calls a worm His friend', the Son of God came to die for them, and 'the Spirit himself beareth witness with our spirit, that we are children of God: and if children, then heirs; heirs of God, and joint-heirs with Christ' (Rom 8$^{16-17}$).

Modern science has also greatly increased man's dominion over nature. Atomic fission and fusion, and flights into space are the most spectacular, but advances in biology and the social sciences are probably more important. Man possesses the key to the genetics of man and he understands something of the working of the human mind and the interactions of men in society. If he succeeds in creating living organisms, he will seem still less inferior to God. The psalmist does not consider the use man makes of this dominion over nature. He thinks of it as the good gift of God. Today we pause and hesitate and question. Man's dominion has always been capable of good and evil, but now the extent of the dominion makes the evil possibilities terrifyingly great. We need to look to the One who did not regard equality with God a prize to be seized, but humbled Himself (Phil 2⁵⁻⁸). The writer to the Hebrews sees that this true dominion is not yet the possession of man but is offered in Christ, who alongside men was made for a little while lower than the angels and died for every man. Now He possesses the dominion (Heb 2⁶⁻⁹; cf. Mt 28¹⁸, 1 Cor 15²⁷). Fittingly, therefore, this psalm has been sung in the Church on Ascension Day.

9-10. 'The needy shall not alway be forgotten'

Almost certainly these two psalms were originally one acrostic psalm. (Other alphabetic psalms are **25, 34, 37, 111, 112, 119, 145**; see note on **37**.) The Greek version treats them as one psalm and this is supported by the absence of a title to **10**. The acrostic cannot be traced throughout the psalm; the D verse is missing and **10**¹⁻¹¹ have either been seriously damaged or have replaced the original alphabetic verses.

The psalms appear to contain a mixture of types with no dominant theme. Leading ideas are the call to thanksgiving, the picture of Yahweh as judge of the nations, a description of the self-sufficient and godless persecutors of the pious, and a plea for the deliverance of the poor and helpless.

9¹³. As it stands this is a prayer for help. Some think this inappropriate at this point and take the verse as an account of Yahweh's past goodness to the psalmist.

10⁴. See *RSV* for a better translation. This is the practical atheism of which all but the most devout are guilty. We act as if God did not exist. We make our plans and take important decisions and do not even allow for the activity of God in our affairs. This assumption underlies almost all politics and international affairs.

10¹⁰. '*He croucheth, he boweth down*'. This is a description of the helpless rather than the wicked—'crushed and prostrate'.

10¹⁷. '*Thou wilt prepare their heart*'. Perhaps, Thou wilt hearken to 'the constancy of their heart'—the heart and mind which are fixed on God and faithful to Him (see **57**⁷, **112**⁷ and contrast **78**³⁷).

The first two verses, which contain five different words for praise, form an attractive call to worship. The singer comes to Yahweh with joyous thanksgiving for His '*marvellous works*'. These works are God's actions in nature and human history. They reveal the character of Yahweh for whom nothing is too difficult (Gen 18¹⁴, Jer 32¹⁷, ²⁷). He acts in nature and in miracles or punishment (Deut 28⁵⁹, Jud 13¹⁹, Job 5⁹, 9¹⁰), but chiefly in salvation, with the Exodus as the pre-eminent occasion (78⁴, ¹¹⁻¹², ³², **106**²², Ex 3²⁰, 34¹⁰). The prophets also look forward to a future marvellous work of coming blessing (Mic 7¹⁵, Zech 8⁶).

Gratitude is a gracious virtue, especially becoming to the Christian, who has seen this future hope fulfilled in a greater work than the psalmist ever knew, the life, death and resurrection of Jesus. Yet simply to have heard of Jesus is of little value unless God's salvation is known now. Gideon found little comfort in God's works in the past when the Amalekites were devastating his land (see Jud 6¹³). The psalmist can offer his thanksgiving with his whole heart because God has saved him (possibly some such vindication as was seen in **7** underlies 9³⁻⁴). God's marvellous works are not past and finished but present and continuing. He saves not only the nation, but also the individual in his private need (see **31**²¹, *RSV*). A living faith requires a present God, and the man who has experienced God's help in his own life can best recount His praises (9¹³⁻¹⁴).

In these psalms, for the first time in the Psalter the 'poor' are mentioned and they appear frequently later. Sometimes they are those without possessions who need gifts from their fellow Israelites (**112**⁹). Often they are helpless against injustice and oppression by the rich (**10**², ⁸⁻¹⁰, 37¹⁴; cf. the denunciations of the prophets, Isa 3¹⁴⁻¹⁵, 10², Amos 2⁶⁻⁷, 8⁴, ⁶). Because of this the righteous king shows his goodness by securing justice for them (**72**², ⁴, ¹²⁻¹³, Jer 22¹⁶). From men they can usually obtain little help and their true source of aid is God. This is the dominant theme in the psalms (see **12**⁵, **14**⁶, 35¹⁰, 76⁹, **140**¹²). The righteousness of God is always revealed most plainly in saving the poor from those who oppress them, and securing for them the justice they are powerless to win for themselves. Since God has this character the afflicted can plead their poverty as a ground to be heard, and when they are saved they rejoice in Him (see **25**¹⁶, **34**², 69²⁹, 74¹⁹, ²¹, **86**¹,

109^{22}). The poor, then, are those in material poverty who are persecuted by the rich, if not always actively at least by being unable to secure their just rights, and who must place their trust in God alone. Thus poverty and piety are closely linked in the psalms. The worker in the factory who so often hears the cry that 'you can't keep high standards around here', and who suffers because he refuses to compromise, would be one modern equivalent to 'the poor' in the psalms.

Perplexity is clearly in the mind of the writer. God is the saviour of the poor. He does not forget their cry (9^{12}). This is his faith, a faith he has confirmed in his own past life—and present experience denies it! The simple optimism of 1 is not for him, for he has seen those set on ruthless greed trampling on the poor and rising to power and influence. They go their own way and leave God out of account—and He seems to have stood aside and justified their atheism. Yahweh the King, whose righteous judgement is sung in the temple worship, is strangely silent in daily life. Why does He not act? Why does He make faith so difficult? He saved the psalmist in the past; why not now? Past experience and temple religion seem irrelevant to this situation. But despite his doubts he continues to hope. The needy will not always be forgotten. Whatever present appearances may be, God must show His real nature in the end, and the psalm concludes on a note of certainty: God *will* hear and do justice to the oppressed.

11. Confidence though the Foundations of Life Crumble

The settled order of society has broken down and there is no longer any firm basis of justice or personal integrity. Wicked men have become accustomed to achieve their own ends by threats and now the psalmist's life is in danger. Even his friends think that the situation is hopeless and that his only way of escape is by flight. But in spite of personal danger he firmly rejects this advice and affirms his confidence in God.

Today this psalm can be well appreciated. The background is similar to that of some colony seeking independence, where patriots and criminals cannot easily be distinguished and law and order are in danger of collapsing completely. Darkness and fear provide a safe cloak for those wishing to remove an upright leader who will not stoop to retaliation and reprisals, and who tries to preserve moral and religious values. The

friends of such a leader see only the risks, and uncertainty
increases their anxiety. What can one righteous man do?
Goodness seems powerless.

The psalmist has a vision that reaches beyond the narrow
limits of earthly society. Yahweh is in His temple—He dwells
in the midst of His people and is not to be driven out by the
evil of the times. And He is no weak human being—His
throne is in the heavens. This God who is present in His world
is the supreme Lord of all. Here is the ground of his confidence. In early times, an innocent man who was accused of
murder and threatened with blood revenge could find safe
asylum if he could reach a sanctuary and cling to the altar
(see Ex 21$^{13-14}$, 1 Kings 1$^{50-1}$). The psalmist finds a surer
refuge in God Himself.

His faith pictures God as universal judge of men, separating
out the wicked and inflicting His fierce punishments upon
them. He will rain down coals of fire and brimstone—a
reminiscence of the fate of Sodom and Gomorrah, used again
to describe divine retribution in Job 18^{15} and Ezekiel 38^{22}.
'*cup*' in verse 6 is a symbol for their fate. In the OT the wicked
drink from this cup their due recompense (see Isa 51^{17}, Lam 4^{21}),
but the righteous find it the cup of salvation (see further **16**^{5}
and **116**^{13}). Perhaps the metaphor goes back to some ordeal
such as is found in Numbers 5$^{11-31}$. The psalmist thinks that
God hates the wicked (verse 5; cf. **5**^{5}), and certainly His
opposition to all that is evil must not be passed over lightly,
for His holy love is inexorably against sin; but the NT gives a
further insight into His ways. The cup is still there, but it was
Jesus Himself who drank it, and He calls His disciples to
follow Him in this way of triumphing over wrong (Mk 10^{38},
14^{36}).

The psalmist, however, cannot end his confession of faith
with fiery judgement. God is righteous and He delights in the
righteous actions of His people. Those whose character is
like His see His face. To worship God in one of the sanctuaries is often described as seeing God (e.g. Ex 34$^{23-4}$—the
Jewish scribes slightly altered the words out of reverence for
God, but this was the original meaning), and **15** and **24** contain a priest's instruction to those who come to worship God
concerning the righteousness required of them. The general
feeling of the OT, however, was that no man is ever fit to see
God, and even Moses was granted the view only of His back

and His goodness (Ex 33$^{17-23}$). In the NT, 'God the invisible appears', though 'veiled in flesh', and the gospel tells of God welcoming sinners. None the less there is still the reverent hesitancy which the Israelites had felt of old. Still it is the 'pure in heart' who see God, and the full vision is reserved for heaven (see Mt 5^8, 1 Cor 13^{12}, Heb 12^{14}, 1 Jn 3^2, Rev 22^4). This is the true blessing, the enjoyment of God for ever. On earth we live by faith, and often it has to be a trust in God despite all the harm which enemies (and friends) can do.

12. ' "I will now arise," says the Lord'

In a time of moral decadence, the faithful receive a word from God.

12^{6b}. This seems to be corrupt. Perhaps we should read, 'Silver refined in a crucible, gold purified seven times.'

12^8. *RSV* takes verse 7 as a renewed petition and this verse as the ground of that prayer, but it comes as something of an anticlimax after verse 6. Some suggest that it is really the comment of a scribe. Others would read in 8b, 'But Thou regardest the sons of men worthless as worms', regarding verses 7–8 as a confession of faith in the promised salvation of God.

The centre of the psalm is the word of Yahweh in verse 5. We may imagine the Israelites gathered together to offer prayer to God. Conditions are much the same as those in **11,** though here the emphasis is laid on lies and flattery. Honesty and truthfulness are no longer treated as the necessary basis of all social and commercial life. A comparison may be made with some modern advertising and much industrial life, where there is little regard for truth and where trade unionist and businessman alike admit that often they are not strictly honest in negotiations or promises, but they have to get the best they can for their members or their firm. It sometimes seems that piety and faithfulness have almost died out (verse 1; cf. 1 Kings 19$^{10, 14}$, Jer 5^1, Hos 4$^{1-2}$).

A prophet then speaks. He is probably attached to the temple and has the task of giving a message from God to the people during the worship. The passages in the psalms which

c

give a message directly from God, or are akin to the words of the canonical prophets, probably come from these cultic prophets (see **14**, **20**$^{6-8}$, **50**$^{7-23}$, **60**$^{6-9}$, **75**, **81**$^{6-16}$, **85**$^{8-13}$, **95**$^{7b-11}$). The present psalm is very similar to Isaiah 33$^{7-12}$, but there is no need to think that it is derived from Isaiah. Both psalm and prophecy are prophetic liturgies used in the sanctuaries. Although these prophets have an official place among the staff of the temple, we must not regard their words as insincere or formal. Their message is a genuine word from Yahweh. He affirms that He will support and save those pious poor who suffer in the harsh life of a corrupt society and are threatened by those who have no thought for God or man but seek only their own advantage. God's salvation is always for those who are oppressed and are unable to save themselves.

The congregation now joyfully acclaims this divine utterance. The wicked speak falsehood and hypocrisy, but God's words are true and reliable. His promise to His afflicted people is no unsubstantial flattery or empty undertaking on their behalf, and they can look forward with confidence to His protection and the downfall of the wicked.

13. 'Hope despairs and yet despair hopes'

This is the prayer of a sick man who feels forsaken by God, yet whose faith finally leads him to sing praise.

13^{2}. '*counsel*'. The word probably means 'sorrows', as it does in Prov 27^{9} and Ecclus 30^{21}.

Sickness and the hostility of enemies are not the dominant features of this psalm. True, the psalmist is sick and near to death, and, like the writer of **6**, he finds that his neighbours point to his illness as a proof of his sin. Death holds great horror, for it will show them to be right in their accusations. But this is not his deepest grief. His first words reveal his piety and his sorrow. God has forgotten him. He cries out in anguish. Will God forget him for ever? It cannot be so. How long must this darkness last? Sickness appears as punishment. His enemy, glad to have this proof of his opinion, looks for the final confirmation. And God does nothing. There is no sound, no answer, no sign that He has heard. Only the man of faith can understand the horror of a silent God.

Four urgent cries, '*How long?*', are followed by three eager
petitions; Look, answer, heal—and then light breaks in. It is
not entirely clear how the two closing verses are to be understood, whether as the assurance of faith, a response to some
word or sign in the temple, or thanksgiving for some blessing
now experienced, but the solid ground of the psalmist's faith
is plain. 'I have trusted in thy steadfast love' (verse 5, *RSV*).
This is the love which has the covenant as its pledge. It does
not waver and dwindle away like man's love, but remains constant, faithful and unchanging. Not even God's salvation is as
amazing as the love which makes Him save. The OT found this
love expressed in the Exodus and confirmed in the covenant.
To the Christian the marvel of God's love is that it led His
Son to travel the way of the psalmist and to know the pain of
feeling that God had forgotten.

Although Christian teaching speaks of this certainty of God's
love in Christ, the individual may still pass through times of
depression that border on despair. He lives among people who
have no faith and is faced with the arguments of those opposed
to the Christian religion. Illness, misfortune or bereavement,
added to the constant struggle to hold to God, may bring him
to where the psalmist stood. There is some comfort in the
knowledge that his very sense of loss shows the important
place God had in his life, but he may have to travel the same
road to a renewed faith. Christ, however, will be by his side,
even if unrecognized as He was on the road to Emmaus
(Lk 24[13–35]; note verse 21, 'we had hoped'—but now hope is
crushed into despair and sadness).

14. God's Help for the Righteous in a Corrupt World

This psalm is identical to **53**, with a few minor variations and
two striking differences. 'Yahweh' in **14** is replaced by 'God'
in **53**, and while **14**[5–6] speaks of Yahweh's protection of the
righteous, **53**[5] describes God's judgement on the wicked. The
psalm was included in two collections which were later incor-
porated into the present Psalter. The collection in which **53**
occurs (**42–83**) avoids the divine name Yahweh out of reverence. **14**[5–6] (=**53**[5]) seem to have suffered accidental or
deliberate alteration.

An exact interpretation is difficult. Verses 1–6 are the word
of a prophet or a lament at the depravity of the times, to which

the prayer in verse 7 is the people's response. The wicked are either foreigners who oppress Israel, or men in high position in Israel (rulers or priests) who wrong the pious minority. The writer seems also to be thinking of the universal sin of men. The religious truths of the psalm can be grasped, however, without giving any precise answer to these problems. In a world where evil is rampant and the godly poor seem to have no protection, God is present. The heavenly Judge stands by the side of the righteous man in his sufferings, and the time will come when He will bring in His kingdom of righteousness and joy.

14⁴. *'who eat up my people as they eat bread, and call not upon the Lord'*. This may mean that they make their living by preying upon the poor, an evil often condemned by the prophets (see Isa 3¹⁴⁻¹⁵, Amos 2⁶, Mic 3²⁻³). The words may be punctuated differently, giving the reading, 'who eat up my people. They eat the bread of Yahweh (either the shew-bread, as priests, or more generally the goodly providence of the earth, cf. Hos 2⁸), and do not call on His Name.' This would suggest that they accept the privileges of religion, or life's blessings, but are utterly heedless of God Himself.

14⁷. *'When the Lord bringeth back the captivity of his people'*. This should be translated, 'When the Lord restores the fortunes of his people' (as *RSV*). It is not a reference to the exile, but looks forward to the good time in the future which God will bring in for those who are faithful to Him (see 85, Job 42¹⁰). This hope was fulfilled in Christ, who made the longings of those who were patiently serving God into a present reality. With Simeon we can now say that we have seen God's salvation (Lk 2³⁰).

The *'fool'* is the churlish man who, like Nabal, lacks all generous feeling, or who, like Amnon, commits gross immorality (1 Sam 25²⁵, 2 Sam 13¹²⁻¹³; cf. Isa 32⁶⁻⁷). The people of Israel are 'foolish' when they forget God with base ingratitude (Deut 32⁶). Folly is that which ought not to be done among God's people (see Gen 34⁷, Jud 20⁶, ¹⁰). Moral evil, not intellectual stupidity or ignorance, is primarily intended, although to neglect God or rebel against His will and

to practise moral evil is foolishness, for in God's world wisdom
lies in serving Him.

This is the practical atheism already seen in 10⁴, ¹¹ (cf.
36¹⁻², Jer 5¹²) which in many ways is more deadly than un-
belief. To believe that God exists and not to worship Him,
to say that God is Creator and ruthlessly to exploit the resources of the world, to call ourselves Christians and never to
allow His will to influence what we do—this is far more
corrupting to the soul than to be unable to believe that there
is a God with an honest mind, while devoting oneself to helping
others and supplying what is lacking in faith by loving service
of men. There is a double problem for faith, the fact that we
who claim to be Christians so often fall far below the standard
of Christ, and the equally surprising fact that many pagans
come so near to that standard. The Utilitarians and the
Churches both brought social reforms in the nineteenth cen-
tury; which were the more effective is an open question.

'*There is none that doeth good*'. Paul quotes the first part
of this psalm to support his assertion that 'all men, both Jews
and Greeks, are under the power of sin', and 'all have sinned
and fall short of the glory of God' (Rom 3⁹, ²³, *RSV*). The
'Biblical theologians' lay stress on the inability of any to
know what is truly good or to do it apart from the Christian
revelation, asserting that to point to high ethical teaching or
spiritual insight in non-Christian religions is to howl with the
wolves. This seems to go beyond the intention of the psalmist
and Paul, to contradict our experience, and to be alien to the
mind of Christ. The psalmist does not teach that mankind
is 'a kind of mass of sin', and that we are all under the 'cruel
necessity of sinning'. He looks out on a corrupt society and
describes how it appears to one who bravely holds to a higher
way (cf. Jer 5¹⁻⁹). In the dark hour, when vice is paraded and
moral decency openly outraged, there are still the few whose
lives are pure, whose minds are noble, and whose faith is
simple and sincere. Paul's description of pagan vices did not
go beyond what is known from pagan writers. Juvenal comments, 'The earth no longer brings forth any but bad men and
cowards. Hence God, whoever He is, looks down, laughs at
them, and hates them.' Yet the circle of Pliny contained con-
scientious, kindly men, faithful to the marriage bond and
considerate to their slaves. It is easy for those who just maintain a desperate hold on goodness in an evil generation to fall

into pessimism, and there are many who slander the grace of
God in their own age.

The psalmist moves far towards this unrelieved gloom, but
he draws back. There are still those who remain true to
Yahweh, who may rightly be called His people. Few in number, with no wealth, persecuted and oppressed, yet God is
with them and He will protect them (14^{5-6}; cf. 53^5). To be
alone but with God at one's side, although invisible, and to
learn to lose with Him, this is the secret of successful living.

Faith evokes prayer, and prayer leans eagerly towards praise.
When God brings in His salvation His people will rejoice.
Christians in time of persecution found the same faith and
the same joy (see 1 Pet 1^{5-9}, 5^{10}).

15. 'Wherewith shall I come before the Lord?'

As pilgrims approach the temple they ask, 'What does Yahweh
demand of those who come to worship Him?' A priest replies
that He requires complete righteousness. See **24** for a similar
liturgy.

15^4. '*In whose eyes a reprobate is despised*'. Attempts have
been made to soften this. Thus some would alter the vowels
and read with the Targum, 'He is despised in his own eyes,
and rejected' (cf *PBV*: 'He that setteth not by himself, but is
lowly in his own eyes'). This expresses an important religious
truth. We cannot force our way into God's presence, confident of our own goodness, but must come humbly before
Him who is holy, conscious of our unworthiness. The contrast here, however, seems to be between the righteous man's
attitude to the 'reprobate' and to those who 'fear the Lord'.
'*despised*' may not reflect the fully Christian attitude, but a
sound society must rest on a true estimate of character. It may
seek to reform the criminal and have a sympathetic understanding of the pressures in his home and local surroundings
which almost drove him into crime, recognizing that many
law-abiding citizens might well have become delinquent in that
situation, but it still needs to express its disapproval of actions
which cannot be tolerated if an ordered community life is to be
preserved. Not to condemn is to condone.
'*He that sweareth to his own hurt, and changeth not*'. The most
natural way of taking the original is, 'He swears to do evil . . .',

which hardly seems possible here, despite Leviticus 5⁴. Hence many alter to, 'He swears to his neighbour . . .', with several ancient versions (as *RV*m). It is probably best to keep the general sense of the *RV*. The good man keeps his word once it is given, even at the cost of personal loss.

The similarity of this teaching to that of the prophets has suggested to some that this psalm gives poetic expression to their words. The priests, however, were responsible for giving instruction in the moral law as well as on ritual and sacrificial matters (see Jer 18¹⁸, where the priests are linked with the Law). One complaint of the prophets against them was that they failed to do this adequately (see Hos 4⁶, Mal 2⁷). It may well be that in this psalm one of the priests gives instruction in the ethical requirements laid upon pilgrims coming to the temple in Jerusalem. Jeremiah may have taken the part of one such priest when he addressed those going into the temple (Jer 7¹⁻¹⁵), and Isaiah 33¹⁴⁻¹⁶ and Micah 6⁶⁻⁸ may be modelled on such liturgies as this. The priest-prophet Ezekiel gives the same kind of teaching when he describes the character of the righteous man (Ezek 18⁵⁻⁹).

Verse 2 sets out the demand in general terms. Those who would come before Yahweh must live a perfect and blameless life (the same word is used of Job in Job 1¹), doing that which is right, dependable and trustworthy, their words matching their thoughts and intentions. The way of Yahweh and His law are 'perfect' (**18³⁰, 19⁷**) and those who come to His house must be like Him.

Verses 3–5 expand these ideas with matters of the everyday. High sounding phrases used in worship must be made very earthy before God accepts them.

First, this blameless way must be seen in dealings with those with whom we live and work. Nothing poisons social relations more than a readiness to pass on the tale that brings discredit to a neighbour. Christian love 'is never glad when others go wrong . . . (is) always slow to expose, always eager to believe the best' (1 Cor 13⁶⁻⁷, *M*).

In society those who worship God maintain true standards, not siding with those who do wrong because they are influential, not neglecting those who faithfully serve God however insignificant or unimportant they may seem. Christian love 'joyfully sides with the truth' (1 Cor 13⁶, *Weymouth*).

The man who has truth in his heart has truth on his lips.

He has learnt to make his Yes mean Yes, and his No mean No, not tempering his words to suit occasions or to secure gain (see Mt 5³⁷).

Further, in all his financial dealings he puts persons before things and men and women before wealth. The commandment against usury (see Ex 22²⁵, Lev 25³⁵⁻⁸) belongs to a simple society where the only occasion for borrowing was in time of dire need. To demand interest on such a loan meant exploiting a neighbour's distress, the denial of the command to love one's neighbour as oneself. This teaching was taken over by the Christian Church. The medieval attitude to economics was over-simple and neglected the pressures of supply and demand, but it expressed the firm determination to apply the Christian faith to the whole of life. By substituting the ideas of the just price and enforced standards of quality for the maxim, 'Let the buyer beware', the Christian ethic was brought into the market place and men were taught that social righteousness is more likely to come from lofty principles than from their absence.

Finally, the true servants of Yahweh will oppose all bribery in the law courts, an evil frequently condemned by the prophets (see Ex 23⁸, Deut 16¹⁹, Isa 1²³, 29²¹, Amos 5¹²).

These are the requirements of those who come to worship, but the psalm ends, not with a demand, but with a promise. God Himself will protect those who possess this righteousness, and will not allow them to fall.

The Christian would wish to add two further thoughts:

(1) The Old Testament priest made stern demands on those who came to worship God; they must be blameless, active in goodness and firm in integrity. With Christ all is of grace, and forgiveness is freely offered to those who have done wrong. None need hesitate to approach the holy God, for He welcomes sinners. Yet faith works by love, and the Christian life is perfected in good deeds. Here and now there is pardon for the blackest sinner—all may come, the only condition is penitence and that is evoked by God's own love freely offered—but the words, 'Come, ye blessed of my Father, inherit the kingdom', were spoken to those who gave food and clothing to the needy, and visited the sick and the prisoners. Christ died in order to present us 'holy and blameless and irreproachable before him', yet we still 'work out our own salvation with fear and trembling'. It is not those who speak about righteousness, or think

high thoughts, or even make elaborate confessions who are sons of God. (See Mt 25[31-46], Gal 5[6], Phil 2[12-13], Col 1[21-2], Jas 1[19-27], 1 Jn 4[20-1].)

(2) 'Yahweh, who may be a guest in Thy tent?' ask the pilgrims—who may enjoy God's hospitality, whom will He welcome into His home? The Israelite obeyed the law, purified himself, and travelled up to the temple, but God in His great love saw that more was needed than a house where men could come to Him, and He Himself came to them as their guest (Jn 1[14]).

16. The Joy of Fellowship with God

Although this psalm begins with a prayer, the dominant note throughout is joyous confidence in God. The psalmist affirms his complete allegiance to Yahweh, and reveals his great delight in being with God. He is certain that nothing can destroy this fellowship.

16[2-4a]. The text of these verses is so corrupt that the meaning is doubtful, but none of the attempted reconstructions is really satisfactory.

16[7]. *'reins'*. Kidneys. In the psychology of the Israelites, the kidneys were the centre of the emotions. Here the word is used of the conscience. Possibly the word translated *'glory'* in verse 9 should be slightly changed to 'liver'. Heart, flesh, kidneys, liver all represent man's inner being—the Hebrews had no word that is the full equivalent of our 'personality'.

16[10]. *'holy one'*. This is a wrong translation derived from the Greek and probably retained because of the quotation in Acts 2. The word means 'pious, godly one', the person who responds to God's love with loyal devotion (as *RV*m, and *RV* in 12[1] and elsewhere).

'corruption'. Better 'the pit' as *RV*m and *RSV*. Sheol, the abode of the dead who continue to exist as shades, was imagined as a cavern beneath the earth and the cosmic waters (see 6).

In view of the general tone of the psalm, the opening petition should probably be interpreted as a request that God will continue to protect the psalmist, rather than as a prayer for deliverance from some trouble which has befallen him.

The psalmist is utterly devoted to God. He shrinks from offering any worship to pagan gods. Yahweh is his supreme good. Perhaps he thinks for a moment of the protection God gives His servants and imagines this rather as the friends of Job did (verse 8b; see Job 5^{17-26}), but God is more to him than any security. Yahweh guides and instructs him, directs his conscience and shows him the way of goodness. He is '*the portion of mine inheritance*', as He was to the Levites who received no land in Canaan, but of whom it was said, 'The Lord is his inheritance' (Deut 10^9; cf. Num 18^{20}). Some men make wealth, power, sensual pleasures their aim, and they obtain their riches, they wield their authority, they enjoy their lusts. The saint seeks nothing but to kneel and adore in wondering love, and he finds that God Himself is his possession. In a time of social security and welfare services and affluence, the word of the psalmist reasserts a half-forgotten order of values. The supreme good for man is to enjoy God. Apart from Him there is no ultimate happiness. To limit our desire to things in the world, good though they are, for God created them, is to find disappointment and unsatisfied longing.

> Should I from Thee, my God, remove,
>   Life could no lasting bliss afford;
> My joy, the sense of pardoning love,
>   My guard, the presence of my Lord.   (*MHB* 389)

Verses 9–11 may go no further than the dismal belief which has been seen in **6**. The psalmist may merely trust that God will save him from premature death and not yet give him up to Sheol. Indeed, this was probably the doctrine he held with his mind. But single-hearted devotion and eager longing lead him to a leap of faith. He has no good apart from God and he never tires of the intimacy of prayer. With a great '*Therefore*' piety refuses to be hemmed in and cramped by doctrine. Fellowship with the eternal God must be eternal. Here is the deep joy of his life. He is not concerned how God will achieve this, whether by immortality or a resurrection or some other way. He knows that '*in thy presence is fulness of joy*'. This is part of the basis of the Christian's belief in a future life. God 'is not the God of the dead, but of the living'. If God is omnipotent and if He loves His human children, He cannot cast them off and forget them. Love does not so lightly lose interest. Omnipotence does not allow physical death to thwart its aims. (See Mk 12²⁶⁻⁷, Rom 8³⁸⁻⁹.)

The NT looked upon verse 10 as a prophecy of the resurrection of Jesus (see Acts 2²⁵⁻⁸, 13³⁵). This was not the intention of the psalmist. The Easter message, however, is the confirmation of his experience and his faith (see 2 Tim 1¹⁰).

17. A Prayer for Vindication

As in 7 and 26, an innocent man who has been wrongly accused looks to Yahweh for acquittal.

Unfortunately, the text is corrupt in several places and the exact meaning is uncertain. *RSV* adopts a few slight changes and is better than *RV*, although still not fully satisfactory.

17¹. '*the right*'. The Greek has '*my* righteousness'—'my just cause'—and this should probably be adopted.

17⁷. '*Shew thy marvellous lovingkindness*', i.e. 'Make wonderful Thy constant love'. Yahweh performed His 'wonderful works' in saving His people at the Exodus and He comes to help the individual with all the wonder of His unwavering love, but He showed the full marvel of that love in Christ Jesus.

The psalmist appears to be spending a night in the temple, waiting on God. After making his appeal for God's verdict he affirms his innocence. The precise charges to which he pleads 'not guilty' are not clear, and it may well be that this psalm was intended to be used by different people as they came to secure their vindication. During his vigil, God can examine his thoughts and He will see that all his intentions are good. He has obeyed God's law and lived according to His will. In the rather difficult original text, he asserts that he is clear of all crimes of violence. Some slightly alter verse 4 to introduce a denial of murder.

Assertions of innocence such as are found here and in other psalms (e.g. 7³⁻⁵, 26⁴⁻⁵, ⁸, ¹¹) may seem to us arrogant and approaching a dangerous reliance upon one's own goodness. While it must be remembered that in these three psalms the psalmist is refuting specific charges, rather than claiming

complete perfection, there is more to this. The stress on righteousness in the psalms shows that to the writers goodness
mattered. They believe that the distinction between right and
wrong is of fundamental concern to God Himself. The latent
danger of trusting in ourselves that we are righteous and setting
all others at nought is always present, and man can only
approach the holy God with the cry, 'God be merciful to me a
sinner' (see Lk 18⁹⁻¹⁴), but without the firm grasp on the vital
need of goodness which is found in the OT there can be no
true sense of sin and no advance into the higher reaches of
religion. Spiritual danger comes when the ideal is limited
to an easily attainable ethic, instead of being the measure of
God Himself, and when we think we have reached this lower
level of goodness and condemn those who happen to transgress
the selection of precepts we have chosen to keep. There is
need to set before our eyes continually the impossible ethic of
Christ. We never reach the point where we can say, 'I have
done all I ought to do', for His word is, 'Ye shall be perfect
as your heavenly Father is perfect.'

The enemies who oppose this psalmist are described much
as in **7,** but he goes further in seeking their overthrow. Verse 14
is open to several interpretations. *RV* regards it as a description of the present prosperity of these enemies. *RSV* takes it
as a continuation of the curse in the previous verse: may they
and their descendants reap the punishment stored up for them.
The Hebrew is very awkward, and minor changes would make
the first line a plea for their destruction. 'With Thy sword slay
them, with Thy hand, O Yahweh. Slay them from out of the
world, destroy them in the midst of life.' Such curses are
found in other psalms (see **35, 69, 109**). They accord ill with
the call of Jesus to love our enemies. A fuller discussion will
be found in a note after **69.**

The climax of the psalm is reached in the last verse. Several
interpretations have been offered of the phrase, '*when I
awake*'. Some suggest that it refers to a daily renewal of
communion with God, others that the psalmist is looking for
a waking experience of God over against a dream. The traditional view has held the sleep to be the sleep of death, and
the psalmist's hope an eager desire for the beatific vision.
More probably, if this is the evening prayer of one spending
the night in the temple, he is looking for vindication and an
experience of God's presence when he wakes the next morning.

Even if a future hope cannot be accepted, the Christian will treasure this verse which expresses the same deep longing after communion with God which was seen in **16**. The psalmist recognizes that only the righteous see God (see **11⁷**, Mt 5⁸, Heb 12¹⁴), but he is seeking the blessing which was given to Moses alone (see Num 12⁶⁻⁸). None reach the purity which fits man to approach God. *'righteousness'*, however, is probably correctly rendered 'vindication'; to the psalmist the word of acquittal and the recognition of his own innocence, but to the Christian the word of forgiveness and his acceptance through Christ.

18. Thanksgiving to Yahweh, Who has saved His Anointed

An outline of this psalm will assist an interpretation of its message:

18¹⁻³. Praise of Yahweh.

18⁴⁻⁶. The great distress of the psalmist.

18⁷⁻¹⁹. God comes from heaven and saves him.

18²⁰⁻⁴. The ground of this salvation—the psalmist is 'righteous'.

18²⁵⁻³⁰. God saves those who trust Him.

18³¹⁻⁴⁵. He saves the psalmist from the attacks of his enemies.

18⁴⁶⁻⁵⁰. Final praise of Yahweh.

The psalm is also found in 2 Samuel 22, with some minor differences. Generally it is better to follow the version in the Psalter, though in a few places 2 Samuel may be nearer the original, such as verse 4, where 'waves' should be read for *'cords'* of death.

18³⁵. *'thy gentleness hath made me great'*. Probably the word translated *'gentleness'* should be read as 'thy answer'—Yahweh answers the call of the psalmist but pays no heed to the cry of his enemies (verse 41). Yet *RV* (cf. *RV*m) might be collected with other 'great mistranslations' (see Job 13¹⁵, *AV*; cf. *RSV*, and note on **96¹⁰**). The Christian remembers that he can become God's heir because Jesus became man's slave.

Some feel that two psalms have here been combined, verses 1–30 being the thanksgiving of an ordinary Israelite who had

been seriously ill, and verses 31–50 the thanksgiving of a
king for victory in battle. Others would treat the psalm as a
unity, and apply the whole to the king, the distress from which
Yahweh has delivered him being either historical or part of a
dramatic ritual in the temple. On the whole the last of these
suggestions seems to account for most of the features of the
psalm, and it certainly provides an exciting basis for preaching
important truths about God and His dealings with men. Since
in this commentary there is little room for detailed discussion,
the cultic interpretation alone will be developed, although it
should be recognized that the alternative views are not to be
casually dismissed.

The king seems to have played a leading role in the worship
of the Jerusalem temple. As king he is the representative head
of the nation, and what he does affects their welfare as well as
his own. The ritual is an effective sign of what God is doing in
the world at large, and when He saves the king it shows that
He is also bringing help and new life to the people. We may
imagine that in the drama the king is attacked by '*enemies*',
who represent not only the national enemies of Israel but also
the forces of sickness, famine, and death. So fierce is their
onslaught that the king is driven back and brought very low.
He feels that the waves of the sea of destruction are lashing
around him, and that he is almost in the world of death already.
In the extremity of his need he cries out to Yahweh for help,
and Yahweh, in His heavenly palace, hears and answers.

The coming of Yahweh is vividly described. With symbol-
ism taken from the thunderstorm and volcano, and imagery
going beyond natural phenomena to the mythology of the
creation of the world, He is depicted as parting the heavens
and descending in majesty and terror. It was like this that
He was pictured at Sinai (Ex 19) and as the battle God in
Judges 5 (see also **97** and Hab 3). Even as earthquake and
smoke, lightnings and hail, are tokens of His appearing, they
veil Him. He is hid amid the thick darkness, for He is God,
mysterious, and not open to man's common gaze.

Those who lived before the coming of our Lord could not
imagine God's appearing apart from glory and pomp and
majesty. When He did come to men, He came humbly,
silently, and almost unnoticed. These great OT theophanies,
however, still bear witness to that side of God's nature which is
too easily overlooked by Christians glibly repeating 'God is

like Jesus'. He is like Jesus, but He is also God. We need to think magnificently about Him, to kneel in adoration before that glory which can only be expressed in words of dazzling light and aweful mystery. He is not bare terror, however, and the incarnation is an even more glorious expression of His splendour.

> *Glory be to God on high,*
> *And peace on earth descend:*
> *God comes down, He bows the sky,*
> *And shows Himself our Friend.* (*MHB* 134)

Thus God, the all-terrible, comes and saves the king in the time of his direst need. When all his own efforts have failed, when the powers of destruction were surging to overwhelm him, God rescued His servant.

Verses 20–4 recall the confessions of innocence which have been noticed in **7** and **17**. He believes that by coming to his rescue God has given him no more than his just due, and, with no suggestion of sin, he asserts that he has fully obeyed God's law and has been faultless in all his relationships with Him. Here, again, the background must be borne in mind. The king is the representative of his people, and the ritual expresses more than his personal and individual attitude to God. Yahweh is a God who requires righteousness from His people and from His anointed. The nature of this righteousness can be seen in **72**. By saving the king, Yahweh not only vindicates him but also reasserts His own moral rule in the world.

The full insight of the Christian revelation cannot be expected in this psalm. The king is saved by God's power, and this salvation is described as his triumph over enemies in battle, the victory ending with the king's opponents being trodden underfoot like the mire of the streets (verses 31–45). There is little desire to redeem these enemies, little love, little sympathy. All is in sharp contrast; life and death, good and evil, the king as Yahweh's anointed and the enemies who are the forces of darkness and disorder. The triumph of Yahweh means the victory of light over darkness and order over chaos and righteousness over sin, a victory which must be won if right and truth are to be vindicated as eternal realities and if Yahweh is truly to be God. Yahweh has made His righteous servant supreme ruler over the nations, over the national enemies of Israel and over the forces of evil who constantly

surge up against the devotees of Yahweh. We find difficulty
in accepting the picture of victory in battle and are offended
by the nationalistic overtones of the psalm. Nevertheless,
while we seek a victory of love rather than of naked power, and
recognize that in this world evil always has some quality of
good mingled with it, we must not weaken in our opposition
to sin. As they press ever deeper into hell, Virgil says to
Dante,

> 'Here pity, or here piety, must die,'

and Dorothy Sayers comments, 'Pity and piety are here mutually
exclusive: it is necessary to acquiesce in judgement if one is not
to become (by sympathy) partaker in the sin.' But this is in
hell. The error is to regard character as irrevocably fixed and
immutable in this life, and to treat our condemnations as the
final judgement of God.

The psalm begins and ends with praise. In the opening
verses, the king heaps together titles for Yahweh which express
His firm, unshakable strength. At the conclusion, he sings the
praises of Yahweh among the nations whom He has quelled.
When one has experienced God's salvation, no other response
is possible.

19. God revealed in Nature and Law

The striking differences in subject, style and poetic rhythm
between verses 1–6 and 7–14 make it almost certain that two
psalms have been joined together here, as they have been in
108 ($108^{1-5} = 57^{7-11}$, $108^{6-13} = 60^{5-12}$). The first part speaks of
the glory of God in the heavens, the second of Yahweh and
His law.

19^3. Day and night chant God's praises, but the meaning of
their hymns is hidden from us. Nature of itself cannot reveal
God (see Wis 13^{1-9}). Only those who have come to know
God through His personal revelation in history and the law
recognize His glory in the heavens.

19^4. '*Their line*'. A measuring line might be thought to mark
out their path, or to set the limits of their possession, but a
similar idea to 'their words' in the next line is required. The
ancient versions read 'their sound' (as *PBV*). This sense might
be obtained by a slight change to 'their voice' (as *RSV*),

although some think that the word itself means 'their chord'
(= 'song'), or 'their flood of speech'.

19⁷. *'simple'*. Not the mentally retarded, but those who are
rather weak-willed and too ready to accept the ideas and ways
of those around them. Yet their minds are open to instruction
and they are teachable. (See Prov 1⁴, ²², 7⁷⁻⁸, 9⁶, ¹⁶⁻¹⁸, 21¹¹.)

19⁹. *'fear'*. The reverence for Yahweh which the law in-
spires. Perhaps a further synonym for the law itself would be
more appropriate; e.g. 'word' as in 119³⁸.

19¹³. *'presumptuous* sins'. Sins deliberately committed in
proud defiance of God. But elsewhere the word means
'proud men' and this may be the meaning here; men whose
self-confident lives might make the psalmist's faith waver,
and weaken his determination to live the good life (cf.
119⁵¹, ⁶⁹, ⁷⁸, ⁸⁵, ¹²²).

(a) Verses 1–6

The writer of the first part of the psalm uses ancient themes to
express his sense of the majesty of God, the antiphonal songs
of day and night and the splendour of the sun. In Babylon
the sun was a god who was worshipped as the 'illuminator of
darkness', who knows the plans of all men and maintains
justice among them. Here the sun is personified as a bride-
groom who has his nuptial tent in the seas under the earth,
and as a hero who strides across the heavens. But God is
the Creator of all and nature shows forth His glory, not its
own.

(b) Verses 7–14

At verse 7 the whole atmosphere changes. The *heavens* declare
the glory of *God*, the *law* is from *Yahweh*. The created universe at its highest can do no more than reveal a distant
divinity, but to Israel Yahweh revealed His name and His
nature and taught them how they should live. The name
Yahweh is joyfully reiterated seven times. He is the personal
God who speaks to men in words they can understand.

This psalmist is no shrivelled scribe, shut up in his narrow
room and peering over his scrolls. To him the law is no dead
book, no stern demand. It is the word of God. We use the

D

phrase so often that the wonder of it is lost. *God's word*—
Almighty God talks to men, teaches them, shows them how to
live. Eagerly the writer picks up different titles for the law and
in varying phrases he describes the blessing it gives. Like
God's 'way' (18³⁰) and His 'work' (Deut 32⁴) this law is
'perfect'.

The mention of '*reward*' in verse 11 should not be misunderstood. This is not the motive for obeying the law, nor does the
psalmist think that by his obedience he puts God in his debt.
The reward is the reviving of the soul, the making wise of the
man whose mind is open to God, the heartfelt rejoicing.

As he ponders this teaching of Yahweh the psalmist realizes
that only through forgiveness can he be made pure and kept
blameless. Penitence is more often provoked by a vision of
goodness, the holy God, the Christ-like man, the ideal, than
by a morbid introspection and searching for our sins. And
he realizes also that men's worst sins are often those of which
they are unaware. We look back with horror at Christian slave
traders and religious mill-owners of the industrial revolution,
but we too are corrupted and blinded by our own age. What
are our '*hidden faults*'? Only as God clears us from these can
we be perfect and innocent of '*the great transgression*', the
sin of rebellion against God which is no less horrible for being
unconscious.

The psalm ends with a prayer that has become so familiar
that it is almost impossible to recapture its freshness. The
psalmist prays that even the lightly spoken words which reveal
the character as studied speech never can (see Mt 12³⁶⁻⁷),
and the inner thought which so often dallies with dreams that
would bring the blood to the face if they were dragged into
the open—that these may be so pure and good that they are
pleasing to God. The prayer is made to Yahweh, who is
addressed as '*redeemer*'. The word has to be stripped of con-
ventional Christian overtones for the wonder of God's love to
shine through. The 'redeemer' is the near kinsman who protects any member of the family in trouble, avenging wrongs,
supporting in poverty and buying back the relative from
slavery (see Lev 25²⁵, ⁴⁸⁻⁹, Num 35¹⁹⁻²⁷, Ruth 2²⁰–4¹⁷).
Yahweh regards Himself as bound to His people Israel by
such ties of kinship as these. This is a favourite theme with
Second Isaiah (see Isa 41¹⁴, 43¹⁴, 44⁶, ²⁴, 47⁴, 48¹⁷). The
incarnation reveals the extent to which God was prepared to

go in carrying out His kinship duties, impoverishing Himself that men might be made rich, being enslaved that men might be freed.

The two parts of the psalm may originally have been distinct, but the present form of the psalm should not be neglected. It is a common fault to think that sources are more valuable than the finished book, and that the original writers are necessarily more inspired than those who selected and edited their words. Isaac Watts brings out the meaning:

> *The rolling sun, the changing light,*
> *And night and day, Thy power confess;*
> *But the blest volume Thou hast writ*
> *Reveals Thy justice and Thy grace.* (*MHB* 802)

Christian tradition adds a further thought, for this psalm is appointed for use on Christmas day. The revelation was not complete until the inarticulate word which nature sang, and which had been tuned to human ears in the law, became man and dwelt among us; until God is seen not as bare deity, not even as the personal Yahweh, but as the Father of our Lord Jesus Christ.

20. A Liturgy for the King

It was usual in ancient Israel to offer sacrifices and prayers for victory before going out to battle (see 1 Sam 7[9], 13[9-12], 1 Kings 8[44-5], 2 Chr 20[1-19]). This psalm is a liturgy for such an occasion.

20[1]. '*The name of the God of Jacob*'. Not a magical incantation as in some pagan religions (see Acts 19[13-16] for the use of '*Jesus*' in this way). The '*name*' represents the personal presence and active power of Yahweh.

20[7]. '*we will make mention of*'. This hardly seems right here and some emend the text to read, 'we are strong in'. However, the word may mean 'boast, place our confidence in' (cf. *RSV*).

20[9]. *RV* follows the punctuation of the original, the King being Yahweh as in Isaiah 6[5]. *RV*m is better, for this is the concluding prayer on behalf of the king.

Verses 1–5 are the prayer of the congregation for the king who has already prayed and offered his own sacrifices to God. The '*day of trouble*' is usually interpreted as the time of an attack by foreign enemies, though the expression could be more general. Some, indeed, regard the psalm as a prayer at the king's enthronement for a prosperous reign. War was a religious undertaking to the Israelites as it was later among the Moslems, and the people sanctified themselves and sought Yahweh's aid before they went out to battle. Victory is described as '*salvation*' (verse 5, cf. *RV*m). The prayer ends with a vow: if Yahweh will grant their prayer, the people will praise Him with songs of thanksgiving and remember that His powerful presence gave them the victory when they set up their triumphal banners.

At this point, some ritual was apparently performed which demonstrated that God had heard and accepted the prayers and sacrifices, for in verse 6 a priest or a prophet stepped forward to announce that Yahweh will assuredly help His anointed king. The contrast which he draws between reliance upon military force and confidence in the power of God is a characteristic of the faith of the prophets (see Isa 31[1-3], Hos 1[7], 10[13], Zech 4[6]).

In the closing verse of the psalm the people reply and reiterate their prayer:

> 'Give victory to the king, O Lord;
>   answer us when we call.' (*RSV*)

A psalm which is set so firmly in the life of ancient Israel may seem to have little to say to the present day Christian, and it is not surprising that some dismiss it as expressing no more than an antiquated belief in a God of battles, though they acknowledge the ardent faith of those who trust in Yahweh alone for victory. Yet one may wonder whether the attitude of modern man is so distant from that of the psalmist, for he too puts his trust in chariots and horses, in H-bombs and rockets—and holds national days of prayer in the darkest days of war! The OT faith in a God who is active in the wider life of the nation and whose interest is not limited to the soul of the individual fills out the NT, where Christians are a minority with no responsibilities for the government of the empire.

21. Yahweh meets the King with Goodly Blessings

In another liturgy the congregation praises Yahweh for the blessings He has given to the king (verses 1–7), a prophet or priest announces further victories (verses 8–12), and the people respond by urging Yahweh to arise and bring in His final judgement (verse 13).

21³. *'prevent'*, in the old sense of 'go before', 'come to meet'. God's goodness is always ahead of our desire for Him.

21⁷. *'he shall not be moved'*. Possibly this refers to God's lovingkindness—Yahweh's love is unshakable.

21⁹. *'in the time of thine anger'*. See *RV*m. Several interpretations are possible: when Yahweh appears in person; when the king comes upon his enemies; in Yahweh's own good time.

There is little agreement about the interpretation of this psalm. Some regard it as a companion to **20,** the thanksgiving after victory. Others, pointing to the hope of future victories in verses 8–12, think it is a prayer before battle, the confidence of the first section revealing the faith which prays believing it has received its requests (cf. Mk 11²⁴). Others again, laying stress on verses 3 and 4, assign it to the anniversary of the coronation of the king. The exalted language of verses 4–6 suggested to early interpreters that this is messianic prophecy, the Aramaic version even rendering '*king*' in verses 1 and 7 by 'king Messiah'. The language may be that of the cult, for it is similar to that of other psalms which have been connected with the autumn festival.

The king can rejoice because he has seen God's victory and has been granted blessing and prosperity through his loyal trust in Yahweh. There is also a forward-looking hope. The victory which has been portrayed in the dramatic ritual is a pledge of Yahweh's final judgement on all those who hate Him and are the enemies of the Israelite king. The description of this victory is in accord with the fierce cruelties of ancient warfare, but their horror is somewhat mitigated when it is remembered that, although these enemies are the national foes of Israel, they represent the forces of evil which are arrayed against God.

These are themes which are taken up in Christianity. Jesus as the messiah showed that loyal devotion to God which the Israelites recognized to be essential, but which the Israelite king never in fact achieved. He received for Himself and made available to all Christians the blessings of 'life' and the joy of being in God's presence. But there is still the future hope of final victory over the forces of evil and of the ultimate triumph of God and His Christ, when all will praise His glorious power (cf. 1 Cor 15$^{24-8}$). Thus, while the psalm was probably not messianic in its original intention, it leads on towards Christ, and it is not inappropriate that it is sung in the Church at Ascensiontide.

By '*life*', in verse 4, more is meant than mere length of days. Although, when there was no true hope of a future life, a premium was placed on a long life on earth (see **61**^{6}, **91**^{16}, 1 Kings 3$^{11, 14}$, Prov 3^2), the bare continuation of existence is no real blessing, as many in the geriatric wards of our hospitals can testify. Life to the Israelite meant life accompanied by health and prosperity (cf. Isa 55$^{1-3}$, where the Greek translation actually adds to 'shall live' the words 'in good things'). Fullness of life like this included fellowship with Yahweh and could only be obtained by obedience to Him (see Lev 18^5, Deut 8^3, 30$^{15-20}$). This approaches the NT idea of eternal life, which is not life without end but life with God, begun in this earthly life and continued beyond time.

Verse 7 touches the heart of religion. Yahweh gave victory to the king because of the covenant which was grounded on His unshakable love and maintained by the king's faithfulness to Him. So it is with salvation. God's love, proved to man in the Cross and as unswerving as it is limitless, alone makes possible man's approach to Him, while man's part is the response of simple trust.

22. 'My God, my God, why hast thou forsaken me?'

One who is ill and surrounded by men hostile to him makes his passionate petition to God and receives the assurance that his prayer is heard. The sufferings seem so intense and personal that this may be the prayer of a particular individual, rather than a lament for the use of any worshipper who came to make his requests known to God, or the king's hymn at his ritual humiliation. The psalmist, like Jeremiah, falls naturally into the common forms of prayer.

22³. Yahweh, the Holy One of Israel, sat enthroned upon the cherubim (see **80¹, 99¹, ³,** Isa 6³, 57¹⁵). According to *RV* the praises form, as it were, His heavenly throne. The words could be taken as:

'Thou art enthroned as the Holy One,
  O Thou Praise of Israel' (cf. *PBV* and Deut 10²¹, Jer 17¹⁴).

22¹². The enemies of the individual are likened to animals elsewhere (see 7², 10⁹⁻¹⁰), but it has been suggested that here demons are intended. In Babylon demons which bring sickness are pictured in the form of dangerous beasts. An incantation addresses the demon Samana as having 'the mouth of a lion, teeth of a dragon, talons of an eagle, tail of a scorpion'. See **91** for further demons.

22¹⁶ᵇ⁻¹⁷. This should probably be:

'They have bound my hands and my feet.
  I recount all my sufferings,
  But they gaze and gloat over me.'

Some suggest further, that verse 15b (slightly altered) should come at the end of verse 16, providing the climax of the ill-treatment: 'And have cast me on the ash-pit of death.'

22²¹ᵇ. *RV*, following the Hebrew, takes this as a sudden flash of bold confidence which leads on to the second half of the psalm, but perhaps the reading of some of the versions should be followed, 'My afflicted self from the horns of the wild oxen.' (Cf. *RSV*.)

22²⁹. '*shall eat*'. If correct, this is a reference back to the sacrificial feasts of verse 26; but it is very probable that the line should be slightly changed to read, '*Surely to Him* shall all the fat ones (the rich and proud) of the earth worship.' The last two lines seem to refer to 'mortal men', though some have seen a reference to those in Sheol who are regarded elsewhere as having no hope of fellowship with Yahweh.

The mysterious cry of our Lord from the Cross seems to have been a quotation from this psalm, and from early times the sufferings of the psalmist were looked upon as a fore-shadowing

of His passion (see Mt 27$^{39-43, 46}$, Mk 15^{34}, Heb 2^{12};
rather curiously verse 16 is nowhere expressly quoted in the
NT). It was natural, therefore, that this psalm should be
chosen for singing on Good Friday. Yet we must go behind
these parallels to see the sufferings and faith of the psalmist
himself. Only then shall we discover their true fulfilment in
Christ.

This is the greatest of the individual laments, akin to Job
and Isaiah 53. We see the wrestlings of a man of faith driven
by his sufferings to the fringes of despair, yet coming through
to a triumphant assurance of God's salvation. Here is the
utter desolation which suffering can bring. Here is the road to
a mature faith. So striking, indeed, is the contrast between the
urgent prayer of the first part of the psalm and the joyful
certainty at the end that some have thought that a lament and
a song of thanksgiving have been joined together. The same
change of tone occurs in other laments, however, and may be
the result of some priestly oracle, or the renewal of faith may
have come to the writer when he brings even his doubts freely
and honestly to God.

In verses 1–21 the psalmist offers his prayer in which despair
almost drives out hope. Desperate are his sufferings. He is
afflicted by serious illness—some fever seems to rack his frame
(verses 14, 15). He is scorned by men and encircled by enemies.
Instead of sympathy, he meets only callous hostility and an
eager anticipation of his death. This sickness is seen as God's
punishment and proof that He has no delight in him (verses
6–8, 16–18). Perhaps he fears the demons who send disease
(verses 12, 13). And, as with many a sufferer, doubts cause
him his greatest grief. He feels he is losing his faith. God
seems to have deserted him. Once he had known intimacy with
Yahweh—He is '*my God*'. Now he feels forsaken.

Two things support him in all his griefs. He looks back into
the history of Israel and remembers that God saved His people
in the past and did not disappoint their trust in Him (verses
3–5). And he remembers that from his birth God has cared
for him (verses 9–10). In the same way, the Christian in times
of doubt and distress, will look back to Jesus, God coming
into the world to save, and to God's love shown to him in the
past. With Luther he may well recall the certainty of the gospel
by remembering, 'I was baptized'—God, who saved the world
in the Cross of Christ, loved me even before I knew Him.

With verse 22 (or 21b) all this changes. The doubts are past. Prayer turns to praise. In the temple, among those gathered for worship, the psalmist sings of God's salvation, and calls them to join him. '*I will declare*' is not a vow, but the introduction to a song of thanksgiving (cf. 66$^{15-16}$). As he worships he offers sacrifice and bids the godly poor share in the festal meal. Those who come to Yahweh's banquet will find full satisfaction and enjoy the rich life of fellowship with Him (verse 26). The Christian's thought naturally moves to the Christian banquet, the eucharist, where his thanksgiving for God's goodness is expressed, where he shares the fellowship with all the godly, and where he knows the presence of the living God which makes this feast an anticipation of heaven.

Pain had fixed the psalmist's gaze within himself and he had seen only his own sorrows, his own sufferings, the persecution to which he had to submit, his desertion by God. Now he turns to embrace the whole world. To his sacrifice he invites the poor. He worships Yahweh eagerly among the great congregation. He looks to the time when foreign nations at the ends of the earth will return to Yahweh and worship Him. His longing is that future generations will praise Yahweh for His great salvation. Some even think that his faith passes beyond death and that he has the vision of those in Sheol praising God. Yahweh is king and His reign extends over all.

Despite the NT quotations, the psalm is not prophecy, but the experience of one who suffered greatly. There is, in fact, no suffering messiah in Jewish thought, and even when Isaiah 53 was given a messianic interpretation all the sufferings were transferred to Israel and only glory was left to the servant. Yet the early Christians were not mistaken when they saw a fulfilment in Christ. When Jesus took the words of the psalmist upon His lips, He showed that He was entering into the lowest reaches of human experience. Not merely pain and death were his, but the feelings of separation from God as well. In a special way He could say, '*My* God'—and He had also to say, '*Why hast thou forsaken me?*' This is the meaning of 'incarnation'. This is the cost of bearing sin. And this is the comfort of the Christian. God did not create a world where sorrow and suffering and death are the lot of man, and then stand and watch their agonizing struggles from a distance that could not be touched by pain. He came Himself and made the 'Why' of the psalmist His own. So that the Christian can say, God

knows, God understands, God shares our suffering with a
sympathy that reaches beyond words and thoughts. And because He is God, the triumph with which the psalm ends is
His too.

23. Yahweh as Shepherd and Host

In a psalm of firm and confident trust, Yahweh is described as
a Shepherd, and as the Host who welcomes one pursued by
enemies, giving him the protection and hospitality of His
home.

23³. '*He restoreth my soul*'; i.e. 'He gives me new life' (*AT*).

23⁴. '*the shadow of death*'. Almost certainly this should be
'deep darkness' (as *RV*m). In the shepherd comparison, the
ravines where wild beasts can lurk in the shadows are meant.
In the religious life, God supports the believer in all troubles,
not only at the hour of death.

The picture of the shepherd is easily treated sentimentally.
In Israel, as in other countries of the ancient Near East, shepherd was a title for the king (see 2 Sam 5², 7⁷, and the messianic
prince of Mic 5⁴). Authority as well as loving care belong
to the figure.

Yahweh is often seen in the Psalter as the Shepherd of His
people (80¹; cf. 74¹, 77²⁰, 78⁵², 79¹³, 95⁷, 100³), and Second
Isaiah tells the exiled Jews that Yahweh will be their Shepherd
to bring them back to their own land (Isa 40¹¹). The greatest
of all these pictures is in *Ezekiel*, where God says, 'Behold I,
I myself will search for my sheep, and will seek them out. . . .
I myself will be the shepherd of my sheep, and I will make them
lie down. . . . I will seek the lost, and I will bring back the
strayed, and I will bind up the crippled, and I will strengthen
the weak' (Ezek 34¹¹, ¹⁵⁻¹⁶, *RSV*). The psalmist boldly makes
this his own. '*The Lord is* my *shepherd.*' God's love for all
men means that He loves each one. Piety transforms the
general truth that God is Shepherd of the nation to the assurance that He is 'my shepherd'. This is very near the NT. Our
Lord not only spoke of God's love as that of the shepherd
tramping across the fells as he searches for one lost sheep, but,
applying the title to Himself, He showed by His life and death

the way the king-messiah shepherds his people (see Lk 15[3-7], Jn 10[1-18], Heb 13[20], Rev 7[17]).

Because God Himself is his Shepherd the psalmist knows that he will lack nothing. Confidence comes from realizing that God is Guide and Protector. This is no easy belief. The psalmist has suffered greatly and many are hostile to him. He has found that God does not prevent trouble coming upon him, but he has discovered that He travels the desolate road by his side (cf. Deut 31[8], Isa 43[2]). In the first three verses he had spoken about God; now, as he remembers the wonder of a God who is at hand when distress crushes him, he addresses Him directly in prayer (*'Thy rod . . . Thou preparest . . . Thou hast anointed'*). Those who have found God real to them in time of trouble cannot talk about Him as if He were out of the room.

All this Yahweh does *'for his name's sake'*. Ezekiel had said that Yahweh delivered the Israelites, not because of any merit they possessed, but in order to show His true nature and power to all the nations of the world (Ezek 20[9, 14], 36[20-23]). In the same way, the psalmist sees that Yahweh watches over him like a Shepherd, not as any reward for his faithfulness, but simply because 'Thy nature and Thy name is Love' (*MHB* 339). In other psalms the phrase *'for his name's sake'* recurs, and each time Yahweh's nature is revealed in forgiving and cleansing sin, delivering from danger, and giving new life (see **25**[11], **31**[3], **79**[9], **106**[8], **109**[21], **143**[11]).

At verse 5, the figure changes from a Shepherd to the rich oriental lord who, like Job, welcomes the stranger and protects him from his enemies (Job 29[12-17], 31[32]). The anointing is the courteous anointing of a guest (cf. Lk 7[46]). The cup is the goblet of wine at the feast, but as a symbol it represents the happy lot of those who come to Yahweh's banquet (see **11**[6], **116**[13]). Again the Christian is reminded of the feast to which Christ invites us as His guests, where the Host, whose head was not anointed when He entered men's houses and who took the slave's part and washed the feet of those who reclined at the meal, gives His own cup of blessing.

The psalmist longs to remain in God's house all his life. The example of Anna (Lk 2[37]) forbids an over-hasty passing off of this as a Levitical confession or an exuberant exaggeration. At the very least it reveals a desire to be in God's presence at every moment of the day, and reflects a delight in

corporate worship which sounds oddly in an age when church
services are condemned as boring and dull. This is the language of the mystics, yet we dare not say that such worship is
intended only for those who have a bent for it (see also **27⁴**,
65⁴ and especially **84⁴**).

Here is faith, alive and vital, radiant in the presence of God.
Others who suffered brought their troubles to God, confessed
their sin, sought relief. This psalmist can only adore. 'He who
believes is not agitated' (Isa 28¹⁶; cf. Rom 8³⁵⁻⁹, Eph 3¹³⁻¹⁹).

24. A Festal Procession to the Temple

As the ark, the symbol of Yahweh's presence, is carried in
procession up mount Zion, this liturgy is sung.

24⁴. '*Who hath not lifted up his soul unto vanity*'; i.e. 'Who
has had no desire for falsehood' (*AT*). '*Vanity*' is what is
transitory, false, or sinful, and sometimes it means false gods
(see **12²**, **31⁶**, Job 15³¹, Isa 5¹⁸). To set one's heart on God
with burning desire is to quench the desire for vanity (see **25¹**).

24⁵. '*righteousness*'; i.e. 'vindication' (as *RSV*).

24⁶. '*generation*'. The word probably means 'lot, destiny'.
It occurs again in Isaiah 53⁸—'and as for his fate, who gave it
a thought?'

'*thy face, O God of Jacob*'. The Hebrew has, 'thy face, O
Jacob'. Either *RV* or *RSV* ('the face of the God of Jacob')
is better, and both have support from the ancient versions.
The phrase means seeking God's personal presence in the
temple worship.

At the great festival the pilgrims who have gathered to
accompany the ark into the temple sing a hymn of praise.
Yahweh is the great Creator. The psalmist uses old world
ideas to express this. Having defeated the waters of chaos,
Yahweh established the ordered world firmly so that it cannot
be shaken. He and no other has done this (verses 1–2; see
further **93**).

Modern knowledge would express the act of creation in
different terms, but does not deny the fact of God as Creator.
The very order of the world and the way men still talk of a

*uni*verse are pointers to this. This is God's world, and He made it a world in which there is almost a waste of beauty, so lavish is His prodigality of goodness.

At this point a spokesman for the pilgrims asks what demands God lays upon those who wish to enter His temple. Such statements, usually requiring ritual purity, were sometimes written on the doors of ancient temples. A priest replies that only those who are morally holy are fit to come into Yahweh's presence. His worshippers must possess complete integrity. Not only outward actions, but also inward thoughts and desires, must be pure. Such men are true to their neighbours and loyal to their God; they do not make falsity their aim, nor take oaths with intent to deceive. These will receive God's blessing—the power to live the full life, with inner happiness and outward prosperity. This blessing, says the priest, is the lot of those who truly seek Yahweh (verses 3–6; cf. **15**).

At once the Christian sees a contrast to his own understanding of God. The priest says that only the righteous may enter God's presence, but Jesus welcomed sinners (Mt 11[19], Lk 15[2]). Yet the Christian also knows that it is the pure in heart who see God (Mt 5[8]), and this psalm should warn us against thinking that God's love treats sin lightly. The ethic of Jesus is an absolute ethic, uncompromising in its demands and requiring nothing less than the perfection of God Himself. The vision of God's goodness and forbearance should lead to penitence, a penitence which confesses its sin sincerely and utterly as do those who expect pardon and not punishment (Rom 2[4]).

The ark now stands before the gates of the temple, and the cry for admittance is raised. To the demand, '*Who is the King of glory?*' the reply is shouted, 'Yahweh, strong and mighty.' The question is repeated and at last the full title of Israel's God is sounded, 'Yahweh of hosts'—the God of the armies of Israel and of the hosts of heaven. The doors are now flung open, and as a victorious warrior Yahweh enters His temple with the pilgrims thronging in to offer their worship.

This shout of triumph is not far distant from the Christian faith, for that too is a victorious faith. Its symbol is an empty cross, its Lord a risen Saviour, for Christ defeated sin, conquered death, triumphed over the spiritual hosts of darkness and now reigns, the King of Glory. Yet even here there is contrast. Yahweh is Lord of hosts—the battle God of Israel.

The NT worships a God whose victory was won on a cross, and the cost of that victory was a night in a garden and a cry of dereliction.

> *Who is this King of Glory? Who?*
> *The Lord that all our foes o'er-came,*
> *The world, sin, death, and hell o'er-threw;*
> *And Jesus is the Conqueror's name.* (*MHB* 222)

The first verse of this psalm will have formed the text of many nature sermons. Yet how far Yahweh is from being only the God of nature. When the Israelite brought his harvest festival gifts to the sanctuary, he remembered the Exodus (Deut 26[1-11]). So here, the Creator of the world is the God who demands moral uprightness from His worshippers. He is vitally concerned with the way men behave, and His demands are ethical, not ritual. He is also the triumphant King—Lord of nature, Lord of morality, Lord of the hearts of those who worship Him. All three parts of the psalm belong together and to separate them is to give a false picture of God.

There is one final thought. Was it perhaps as Isaiah went up with the pilgrims at this festival, as he heard Yahweh praised as the King, the Lord of hosts, whose glory is the fullness of the whole earth (verse 1), and who requires holiness from those who come to worship (verses 3–6), that he suddenly saw the meaning of this for himself, bowed down in penitence and found cleansing and a mission (Isa 6)?

25. A Prayer for Pardon and Guidance

This is a lament in the form of an acrostic, and is a companion psalm to 34 which is an acrostic thanksgiving (on acrostics see 37). Not only have both psalms the same peculiarities of structure (no W verse and an additional P verse at the end), but the thought is similar. They may be by the same author.

The acrostic form to some extent hinders a fully logical development of the thought and there is some repetition. The main divisions have been seen in: verses 1–7, a prayer for help, guidance and forgiveness; verses 8–14, reflections on the character of God and the blessedness of those who fear him; verses 15–21, further petitions for deliverance; verse 22, a prayer for Israel, which may be additional to the original psalm.

25¹⁻². To fit the acrostic, the second verse should begin at 'in thee', and some Greek manuscripts join 'O my God' to the end of the first verse. It has been suggested that verse 1 was originally something like:

'Upon Thee, O Yahweh, I wait,
I lift up my soul to (=set my desire upon) my God.'

25¹⁷. Almost certainly the words should be read as *RV*m; both lines are a prayer for deliverance.

25¹⁸. Both this verse and the next begin with R. Many different suggestions have been made to provide a Q verse, either by replacing 'Consider' by another word of similar meaning, or by reading '*Confront* my enemies' in verse 19.

As with other alphabetic psalms, it is best to pick out the leading ideas of the writer. Almost every verse contains important religious truths.

(1) *The character of the good man and his reward*

Although the psalmist does not describe his ideal of the godly man, it shines through all his words. Eagerly he longs for God (verse 1). His constant attitude is of trustful waiting on Yahweh, looking eagerly for Him (verses 2, 3, 5, 21). So great is his desire for God that his eyes are ever turned to Him in prayer (verse 15; cf. 123¹, ²).

Alongside this eager longing there is reverent awe, for he knows that Yahweh is God, and he remains obedient to His covenant and to His testimonies, the solemn duties involved in the acceptance of the covenant (verses 10, 12; cf. 132¹²). Religion is no emotional feeling towards a father substitute, but it involves obeisance at the foot of the Divine Mystery and stern acceptance of His ethical demands.

The psalmist expects those whose lives are centred on Yahweh to receive blessing in this life. They themselves ('*His soul*') will be prosperous and their children will have permanent possession of their land (verse 13). Yet he realizes that no material gifts can satisfy the heart that is set upon God. He Himself is its sole reward. 'Those who reverence the Eternal have his confidence'—He grants them intimacy with Himself (verse 14, *M*; cf. 55¹³⁻¹⁴, Amos 3⁷, Jn 15¹⁵). The tragedy of spiritual shallowness is that we try to serve God as faithful slaves in the hope of being given His blessing, and we fail to discover what it means to be His friends.

(2) *The character of God and His dealings with men*

God is noted for His '*tender mercies*' and His '*lovingkindness*' (verses 7 and 10). Tender mercies are the feelings of a mother for her child, to whom she is closely linked with ties of love and whose welfare she always seeks without overlooking his faults (cf. Isa 63[7-14]). Lovingkindness is one of the great words of the OT. It expresses God's firm, unwavering love, which is loyal to the covenant and constant in its care of His people, and which passes beyond obligation or duty to a gracious affection for Israel. With it is joined God's '*truth*', His faithfulness to His promises and to His covenant (verses 5, 10). The psalmist also speaks of the '*goodness*' of Yahweh, that innermost character of God which can be seen when His glory is hidden from man (verses 7 and 8; see Ex 33[19]). This was the God who revealed Himself to Moses and to whom the whole of Israelite history bears witness (cf. Ex 34[5-7]).

It would be valuable to trace these four words through the Psalter, to see how they are worked out in Yahweh's relations with men. In this psalm we find that He forgives sin and guides the meek—those who have no confidence in their own wisdom but are humble enough to accept the teaching of God (verses 7 and 9; strange that we have to be humble to accept the teaching of Him who made the universe). Especially to be noted is Yahweh's care for sinners (verse 8), an idea which the Greek translators found so startling that they toned it down by rendering, 'those who go astray in the way', though the Christian remembers that it was while we were still sinners that Christ died for us (see Rom 5[8]).

(3) *The psalmist's prayer*

Like those who assert their innocence in the face of false accusations, this psalmist prays for deliverance from his enemies. He looks for relief from his loneliness and trouble. And as in those other laments he puts forward, as a ground for his plea, his sufferings, the bitter hatred of his enemies and their gleeful triumph should that plea fail (verses 2–3, 16–19).

Unlike those psalmists, however, he knows that he is not guiltless. He has sinned, not only with the light errors of

youthful folly, but with a deliberate rejection of what he knew
to be right. To rebel against a loving God is to incur the great
guilt of ingratitude (see Isa 1²⁻³). The only ground on which
forgiveness can be sought for this lies in the character of God
Himself, loving, merciful, and good (verses 6–7, 11). We cannot plead any extenuating circumstances, the weakness of our
will, the suddenness of the temptation, the enticements of
others. We can only say, 'For the sake of Jesus Christ'.

Knowing his waywardness he prays for guidance. May
Yahweh show him His ways (verses 4, 8, 9, 10, 12). The way of
Yahweh is the life which He guides by the instruction of His
law. This teaching is no burdensome demand which cramps
the personality and forbids all pleasure. It is the way which
leads to the full life (see **119¹⁻³**, Deut 10¹²⁻¹³, 26¹⁷⁻¹⁹). It is
God's will which He graciously reveals to men (**103⁷**, Gen 18¹⁹,
Ex 33¹³). In the messianic age, foreign nations will come to
Zion to learn God's ways and receive His law (Isa 2³). But
the law, however perfect (cf. **18³⁰**), could never bring men to
obedience and, as **67²** shows, God's way is His salvation. The
full significance of the term is found in the NT, for Jesus is
Himself the Way. It is He who brings man to obedience and
to God (Jn 14⁶, Heb 9⁸, 10²⁰).

26. 'I wash my hands in innocence'

This psalmist, like the writers of **7** and **17**, comes to the temple
to seek God's vindication of his innocence (cf. 1 Kings 8³¹⁻²).

26². '*Try my reins and my heart*'. The reins (kidneys) were
thought to be the seat of the emotions, as the heart was of the
thought and will.

The psalmist asks Yahweh to give him justice and acquit him
of the accusations which were being levelled against him.
Conscious of his innocence, he lays his inner being open to
God's searching gaze. As in **7** and **17**, his words must not be
regarded as expressing a self-righteousness which can see no
wrong in itself, but are the repudiation of specific charges.
He can come to God confidently because he has trusted Him
and, relying on His constant love, has experienced His faithfulness in his daily life.

After affirming that he has had no dealings with evil doers,

E

he performs a ritual hand-washing expressive of his innocence
(cf. Deut 21[6], Mt 27[24]) and joins a procession round the altar.
It has been suggested that the '*vain persons*' of verse 4 are
sorcerers and necromancers and that this is the charge laid
against him (see Deut 18[10-12]). Because his conscience is
clear, he can take part joyfully in the temple worship.

Verses 9–11 contain a further plea to Yahweh not to destroy
him as He destroys the guilty—murderers, those harbouring
evil designs (the word is often used of sexual sins, as in
Lev 18[17], 19[29], Job 31[11]), and those who wrong the innocent
and the poor by taking bribes (see 5[6], 55[23]).

The psalm ends with the certainty that Yahweh has heard
the prayer.

Some of the ideas in this psalm belong to the distant past—
the oath of innocence, the whole ritual of divine vindication,
and the belief in God's fearful retribution by sudden death—
and other phrases express ideas which appear to be so unchristian that it is difficult to fit them into Christian worship.
Yet isolated verses are valuable. Like the psalmist, the Christian needs to keep God's grace constantly before his eyes
(verse 3), and he too will wish to recount with glad thanksgiving the wonders of God's love, both in the life of Christ
and in his own experience (verses 7 and 12). And there is the
important idea underlying the whole psalm that our actions
in what we call secular life are of concern to God.

27. Confident Faith and a Believer's Prayer

Two psalms seem to have been joined together as in **108**, a
psalm of glad confidence which reminds us of **16** or **23**, and
the urgent prayer of one falsely treated as an evil-doer and
deserted by all his friends. Those who regard the psalm as a
unity point to links between the sections; the enemies and trust
in Yahweh are common to both.

27[2]. '*to eat up my flesh*'. *RSV* takes this to mean slander,
but it may be a vivid phrase for the hostility of the psalmist's
enemies (cf. 7[2], 17[12]).

27[8]. A literal translation is, 'To Thee my heart has said,
"Seek (plural) my face"; Thy face, Yahweh, I will seek.' This
can hardly be the correct text and some emending is needed,
though *RV* requires fairly big changes.

27¹³. As *RV* italics show, '*I had fainted*' is not in the original. The Hebrew might mean, 'O, had I not believed . . . '. The man of faith sees the hopeless despair of being without God and flinches (see Eph 2¹²). There is some doubt about the word 'unless' and *RSV* deletes it. Others make a slight alteration to read, '*And* I did *not* believe . . .' (cf. **31²²**).

(a) Verses 1–6

The confident trust of these verses is not the reckless exuberance of youth or the comfortable belief of those who have never had to face trouble. It has been won after a life of hard experience. Amid the attacks of opponents—and the military metaphors need not be restricted to armed warfare—the psalmist has found Yahweh a stronghold and refuge. Secure in Him he has no fear. So Paul, five times beaten by the Jews, three times given Roman floggings, stoned, shipwrecked, in constant dangers as he travelled preaching the gospel, could say, 'I am convinced that there is nothing . . . in all creation that can separate us from the love of God' (Rom 8³⁸⁻⁹, *NEB*).

The psalmist speaks of Yahweh as light, salvation and stronghold. Light is a relatively rare title of God in the OT. It suggests His guidance (cf **43³**; the law is a light in Prov 6²³, cf. **119¹⁰⁵**) and His salvation (cf. **36⁹**, Isa 51⁴, Mic 7⁸; the Aramaic translation interprets Isa 60¹ by, 'Arise, shine clearly, Jerusalem, for the time of thy salvation has come'). Both the Messiah and the Servant bring this light to the gentiles (Isa 9², 49⁶). When Jesus declared Himself to be the Light of the world, He meant more than that He revealed the truth about God. He brings God's salvation to men (Jn 8¹², cf. Jn 1⁹, 2 Cor 4⁶, 1 Jn 2⁸).

Secure in God, the psalmist has only one request; that he may have continual fellowship with Him. He expresses this as a longing to live for ever in the temple and there to experience the 'pleasantness', the gracious kindliness, of Yahweh and to receive tokens of His goodness (see **73** for another psalmist who found God in the temple). Probably he does not envisage becoming a priest but, like Brother Lawrence, he wants to be as near God, wherever he is, as if he were in His sanctuary. Those who know God in the everyday, however, are eager to come to the sanctuary and worship Him with joyful praises.

(b) Verses 7–14

At verse 7 earnest prayer begins. It may be that the psalmist, like the writers of **7, 17** and **26,** is seeking divine acquittal. The enemies are those *'false witnesses'* who accuse him of some wrong. Even his family think him guilty and have cast him off. His sole means of justifying himself is to receive God's word of vindication. Verse 13 probably expresses his faith in God in spite of all, though on one reconstruction it shows the depths to which the hostility of those around him has brought him—he could hardly believe that he would ever again experience God's goodness.

Then comes the word of a temple priest. Yahweh has heard his prayer. Let him trust and remain confident (verse 14).

Even if the two parts of this psalm were originally separate, there is significance in their being brought together. When all is dark and men doubt him and turn away with bitter accusations on their lips, when a man's hold on God falters and he can only wait, seeking God's face though it seems to be turned away from him, the firm confidence of another may support his own wavering faith and sustain him in his prayer.

28. 'If thou be silent'

This prayer for help is marked by a deep sense of the horror of a silent God.

28². *'thy holy oracle'*. As *RV*m shows, the Holy of Holies, the innermost shrine of the temple, is meant. In the pre-exilic temple this contained the ark; in post-exilic times it was empty, as the Roman general Pompey discovered when he entered it. Although a holy place may help us to fix our minds on God and thus may aid our prayers, He is not confined to a shrine. And He will no more be found there by the unspiritual than in any other place (see 1 Kings 8).

28³. *'Which speak peace with their neighbours'*; i.e. 'Who offer friendly greetings to their neighbours' (*AT*).

28⁸. *'their strength'*. It is better to read with some of the versions, 'a strength unto his people' (as *RV*m).

The trouble which afflicts the psalmist is not clear. He may be gravely ill (see verse 1), or be persecuted or falsely accused of wrong-doing (cf. 26⁹⁻¹⁰). It has been suggested that both this psalm and 26 are prayers in a time of a plague which carries off both wicked and good.

More important than the nature of the distress is the reaction of the psalmist. He says that he will be like those who go down to Sheol if God is silent (for the '*pit*' see 30³, 88³⁻⁷). Silence probably signified God's failure to give a favourable answer through the word of a prophet or a priest in the temple. He feels that God's silence would be death to him. Some of the Victorians found their faith wrested from them by the discoveries and theories of science, and they felt the chill blackness of an empty universe, a world without God. Today many seem to care little whether there is a God in heaven or no, and go on their way with a chirpy whistle and a shrug of the shoulder. It takes little insight to see which is the more profound, the psalmist's shiver or modern man's carefree cheerfulness.

The call for retribution on the wicked appears to be quite out of accord with Christian thought or even the highest levels of the OT. It is clear that in the same way that God has no pleasure in the death of the wicked, but desires that the wicked turn from his way and live (Ezek 33¹¹; cf. 1 Tim 2⁴, ⁶), so we should seek their redemption. Yet three things may be said of this passage. (1) The special sin condemned here is the cruel hypocrisy which is envious of others and looks for ways of secretly harming them. This can evoke little sympathy. (2) The psalmist's petition is not a vindictive desire for revenge, but a firm stand for morality (see on 5, 15⁴ and 18). (3) While the psalmist certainly intended simply that God would punish the wicked as they deserve, his words may have a richer meaning for us. 'Requite them according to their work' (verse 4, *RSV*). The punishment of sin is not some unrelated pain, but is the sin itself, stripped of its glamour and seen with disillusioned eyes for the nasty thing it really is. One experiment with delinquent children has been to leave them together to do all the damage and injury they want, until they discover the hell they have made for themselves.

Verses 6–7 may be the thanksgiving after deliverance or a memory of past help from God, but more probably they are the response of the psalmist to a word promising relief from his trouble, spoken by a temple official (see on **3**). The heart of one who knew the blank pain of addressing a silent God leaps with joy. Yahweh has heard! He had trusted God and now God has answered that trust and helped him. Joyful praise is all his thought.

The last two verses may be an addition to fit the psalm for use in corporate worship. God who is the support of the people and the defence of the king is asked to watch over them like a shepherd (cf. Isa 40[11]). The liturgical character can be seen in the use of phrases from these verses in the responses in matins and in the *Te Deum* (in a version taken from the Vulgate). If the verses are by the original psalmist, it would show that the truly pious man who has been helped by God immediately turns his thoughts away from himself to others.

29. The Majesty of God

This powerful hymn of praise seems to come from very early in Israel's history. It is similar to Canaanite hymns which have been discovered in Syria, and some suggest that it may even be a hymn to Baal which has been adapted for the worship of Yahweh. The reference to the Sinai tradition in verse 8, however, shows that it was not taken over unchanged, and it may well be Israelite in origin.

29[1]. '*sons of the mighty*'; i.e. 'sons of gods', or 'of God'. These are the divine beings who form Yahweh's heavenly court (see 89[6], Job 1[6], 2[1] and the notes on **82**).

29[2]. '*in the beauty of holiness*'. Another inspired mistranslation! Holiness is attractive. But the meaning is probably 'in holy array' (*RV*m). Those who come to worship Yahweh must be fittingly clothed (cf. Ex 28[2], Mt 22[11]). Or this may be descriptive of Yahweh—'Bow down to Yahweh in His holy splendour'.

29[6]. '*Sirion*'. The Phoenician or Canaanite name for Hermon, as archaeology has confirmed (Deut 3[9]).

29[9]. '*And strippeth the forests bare*'. Probably the words really mean, 'And causeth kids to be brought hastily to birth'.

It is characteristic for hymns of praise to open with a call to the congregation or the choir to praise God. Such a call is too narrow for this psalmist who is going to sing the majesty of Yahweh. The lesser gods of His heavenly court are called to praise Him for His glory and power and to offer their worship (verses 1–2). The Christian, too, feels his own voice too weak and the great congregation too small to sing God's praises, and he joins with 'angels and archangels and all the company of heaven' to 'laud and magnify Thy glorious Name'.

The main section of the hymn describes Yahweh as the great God of the thunderstorm and earthquake. The 'voice of Yahweh', repeated like seven thunder claps, echoes over the waters, majestic and terrible. In Lebanon, it shatters the lofty cedars; the very mountains skip like the calves of the fierce wild ox, the silent desert is terrified, the fallow deer and mountain goats, fearful of the storm, untimely bring their young to birth. And in the temple His worshippers cry '*Glory*' (verses 3–9).

The two final verses show that the psalm is not simply a description of a thunderstorm, but is linked with the religious life of Israel. Yahweh is enthroned victor over the flood— the cosmic sea that gives rain and springs of water, and without which no crops can grow, and no creature live, yet which can sweep away man and beast if it is not controlled by Yahweh (see **24, 93**). The psalm may have been sung at the great autumn festival, when the wheat and grape harvests had been gathered and the people looked forward to the rains which would give fertility for the coming year. With the rains Yahweh will sustain His people and secure their welfare.

'*Peace*' has a wider meaning than the English word. It can mean absence of war, and such peace is one of the greatest blessings offered to mankind (see Isa 9[6-7], Mic 4[3-4]), yet it does not mean only this, for David can enquire after the 'peace' of the war (2 Sam 11[7], *RV*, 'how the war prospered'). Peace is no starved, negative thing which happens to appear when warring passions are dispersed. It is full of the wealth of material and spiritual well-being (see Ezek 34[25-31], Zech 8[12]). 'Peace be with thee' was the common greeting (it is the Arab's 'Salaam'), and while no doubt, when used conventionally, it could have as little meaning as our 'Good-bye' (= God be with you), it contains all the promise of divine blessing (see 2 Sam 18[28]; contrast the priestly blessing of Num 6[24-6]).

When Jesus tells those whom He has healed to depart into
peace (e.g. Lk 7[50], 8[48]), or when His disciples speak peace to
the house where they are lodging (Lk 10[5–6]), this richer sense
is seen. This is the peace which Jesus gave to His disciples
(Jn 14[27]), and which is one of the fruits of the Spirit and belongs
to the Kingdom of God (Rom 14[17], Gal 5[22]).

30. Thanksgiving for Recovery from Sickness

A man who has been ill comes to the temple to express his
thankfulness to God. He remembers his suffering and his
prayers (verses 6–10) and calls on all who serve God with
loyal devotion to join him in his praises (verses 4–5).

30[4]. *'saints'*; i.e. those who are devoted to God. The word
does not necessarily include moral goodness, though those
who are dedicated to God and loyal to the covenant will seek
to obey His law and to respond to His love by imitating it in
their own lives.

30[5b]. The Hebrew is very terse, but the sense is probably as
RV. God's anger brings suffering, but lasts only a short time.
His favour brings life in all its fullness. *RV*m takes the verse
in the sense of Isaiah 54[7–8]. With either meaning the stress is
on the greatness of God's goodness and the blessing this brings
to man.

30[7a]. This is usually taken to express Yahweh's protection
of the psalmist in the past, though the precise meaning is
uncertain. It has been suggested, however, that the words
really mean, 'O Yahweh, in Thy pleasure Thou didst cast down
mighty mountains.'

The ideas of this psalm are similar to **6**. Sickness is regarded
as punishment sent by an angry God, and the psalmist's
enemies point to it as proof of his guilt. Illness is described
as in part the weakness of death, and the psalmist feels that
he has already entered some way into Sheol, where there is
no fellowship with Yahweh and no opportunity to praise
Him.

As he recalls his sickness, he realizes that when all had gone
well with him he had fallen into a self-sufficient confidence

which could not imagine that any trouble would ever come to him. If verse 7a speaks of God's loving care which had sustained him, this may slightly ease the sinfulness of his self-confidence, but he had come very near to the thoughts of the wicked in **10⁶**. Even his prayer in his distress was concerned more with himself than with God. He had reminded Yahweh that those in Sheol cannot praise Him and that He would lose a worshipper if He did not heal him.

The singers of Israel can speak to our heart because they are so human. We, like this psalmist, act most of the time as if we were immortal, and through that strange quirk of the human mind which makes us think that though distress and sickness come to others they will never afflict us, we always have to face trouble with spiritual resources that have been drained dangerously low. If we smile at the naïveté of the psalmist's prayer, we should remember that most of our prayers are as childish. Indeed, in times of trouble no prayer can really go beyond his final plea, 'Hear, O Lord, and be gracious to me! O Lord, be thou my helper!' (verse 10, *RSV*).

But the grief and the illness are now past. God has healed him. His sorrow has been turned into dancing. His inner being ('*my glory*', see **16⁹**) pours out its praises. He can never cease to express his thanksgiving. Despite his forgetfulness of God and his reliance upon his own resources, God's anger had only lasted for a moment and sorrow was a lodger who had left with the dawn.

While we cannot accept that God vents His anger by sending disease and pain, the whole gospel is the proclamation of the immensity of God's love. Though we are heedless of His presence and will not credit that without Him we can do nothing (Jn 15⁵), He still maintains us in prosperity and gives more joy than sadness. We should give thanks to Him unceasingly; yet He still blesses us, as Christ healed the ten lepers though only one returned to give thanks (Lk 17¹¹⁻¹⁹).

31. Faith prays and finds Deliverance

Urgent prayer, quiet trust and glad thanksgiving, mingle in this psalm. It is, therefore, no wonder that some divide it into two or even three distinct poems (verses 1–8 and 9–24, some further separating off verses 19–24). Although verses 1–8 have

the appearance of a complete individual lament and a fresh
start is made at verse 9, it is perhaps best to take the psalm as
a whole as a prayer offered in the temple by one in deep
distress, who receives the assurance that he has been heard.
(Some token of Yahweh's favour must have been given
between verses 18 and 19.) The special need of the psalmist
is uncertain. There are hints of sickness and stronger signs of
false accusations and persecution.

31⁶. '*I hate*'. It is better to read with the ancient versions,
'Thou hatest', since the psalmist is contrasting his own
trust in Yahweh with those who worship idols.

31⁷. '*wasteth away*'. Probably 'grown dim' (as in **6⁷**).

31¹⁰. '*iniquity*'. Some of the versions make a very slight
change to read 'misery' (as *RSV*). This is better. There is no
other hint of a sense of sin in the rest of the psalm.
  '*are wasted away*'. Probably the word means, 'are diseased'.

31¹¹. '*exceedingly*'. The word should probably read as a
noun, 'grief'.

> 'To my neighbours a grief,
>   and a fear to mine acquaintance.'

31²¹. '*in a strong city*'. A small alteration would give, 'in a
time of distress'.

The tone of the psalm is set in verses 2–3. 'Prove Thyself to
be what I know Thou art.' This is the mark of believing prayer.
The psalmist lovingly sets out the character of Yahweh. He is
the rock, the fortress and the refuge of those in distress,
faithful to those who entrust themselves to Him and eager to
vindicate all who are wronged. He lays up a wealth of goodness for those who worship Him. Above all is His unwavering
love which is both the ground of the psalmist's prayer and the
joy of his deliverance. This is the One whom he can call '*My
God*', and to whom he can pray, 'As thou art God, oh lead me'
(verse 3, *M*).
  Yet distress comes. Enemies seek to entrap him and they
plot his death. Sorrow and disease have weakened his body.

His friends desert the one they regard as a great sinner and ignore him as if he were already dead. In much the same way Jeremiah knew the whispered plottings and terror on every side. He too was denounced by his friends (Jer 20⁷⁻¹³). And like the psalmist, the prophet has not learned the love which can seek the good of its enemies, but he looks for vengeance on those who persecute him (verses 17–18; cf. Jer 11¹⁹⁻²⁰, 17¹⁷⁻¹⁸, 18²⁰⁻³). Even the most sensitive soul has regions where the conscience is blunted and the spirit blind.

Faith and affliction—the psalmist links them by committing his life to God and seeking help from Him who alone can deliver (cf. 10¹⁴). '*Into thine hand*'. And his prayer was heard. He discovered the broad reaches of God's salvation. In his desperate plight he saw the miracle of God's love.

'*Into thine hand*'. Luke tells that these were the last words of our Lord on the Cross (Lk 23⁴⁶). He had already prayed that He might be saved from the suffering that had to be His. He had tasted that suffering and drained its bitterness to the dregs. Even His faith failed. But His trust never wavered. '*Into thine hand*'. And Christians down the centuries have taken the psalmist's words upon their own lips and died in the confidence that none could snatch them from God's hand (Jn 10²⁸⁻⁹; cf. 2 Tim 1¹², 1 Pet 4¹⁹). The prayer of the psalmist was for life and he sought, and found, a present deliverance. The word of Jesus enables those to pray this prayer who do not find release, but to whom can now be said with more assurance than the psalmist ever knew, '*Be strong, and let your heart take courage*'.

32. The Happiness of the Forgiven Sinner

With joyful thanksgiving the psalmist tells of the forgiveness he found when he confessed his sin to Yahweh.

32⁶. '*in a time when thou mayest be found*'. See 69¹³, Isa 55⁶, Jer 29¹³. But the Hebrew is simply 'in a time of finding; only . . .' (or 'surely'), which might be taken as the time when Yahweh searches out sin (as *RV*m). Some alter to, 'at a time of distress' (as *RSV*).

32⁸ᵇ. The Hebrew may mean, 'I will direct my eye upon thee'.

After a short introduction, in which he declares the happiness which follows God's forgiveness (verses 1–2), the psalmist recounts his experience. Though he knew he had sinned, he had stubbornly refused to confess. But he could find no rest, only anguish of mind and bodily sickness (verses 3–4). He was thus led away from his proud defiance to seek forgiveness, and he discovered the miracle of grace (verse 5). He cannot hide this within his own heart, but calls on others to join him in his new-found peace with God (verses 6–7). Verses 8–9 contain instruction such as the wise men gave. Perhaps the psalmist is seeking to save others from the sorrows he has passed through and urges them to accept God's kindly leading, or a fatherly priest gives advice to the worshippers out of a lifetime's experience. More probably this is the word of Yahweh Himself. He will give instruction in His way and will follow those who return to Him with His all-seeing providence (cf. 33[18], 34[15]). God's love is sure—let those whom He has justified rejoice and shout for joy (verses 10–11).

This thanksgiving for forgiveness was a favourite with Augustine, who had it written on the wall by his bed as he lay dying. Luther placed it beside **51** and **130** as the psalms nearest to the gospel. Yet some find grave limitations in it. These objections may speedily be pushed aside. It may be that the sufferings which came to the psalmist included physical sickness (see Mk 2[1–12] for an illness which sprang from a sense of guilt), but this is only a minor trouble to him. It is to be noted that he makes no request for healing. Verse 10 is said to contain merely the orthodox doctrine of retribution, although the good fortune which comes to those who trust in Yahweh is the fact of being surrounded by His love. It has even been asserted that confession is made a good work which achieves forgiveness! It is better to turn to the insights into the nature of confession and forgiveness which the psalm contains.

The psalmist realizes the seriousness of sin. One man may think that God is no more troubled by our sins than we are by a group of puppies tumbling over each other on the hearth-rug, or snapping at each other in play; another speaks of the 'sin obsession' of many Christians. This psalmist knows sin for the ugly thing it is—missing the way and falling short of what we should be, moral perversion and guilt, and deliberate rebellion against God. Perhaps too much stress should not be laid on the three words he uses for it. Etymologies can be fascinatingly deceptive. We do not readily link 'Forgive us our trespasses' with 'Trespassers will be prosecuted', and it is by their emotional overtones that we distinguish our synonyms rather than their origins in history. Nevertheless, his horror of sin is real.

And his confession is real. The threefold description of sin is matched by a threefold confession (compare verses 1–2 with 5). Masters of the spiritual life speak of the dangers of dishonesty in confession. To use extravagant words whose value we write down even as we speak them will not deceive God, even if it deceives ourselves, and to pray, 'O Lord save—but not yet', is no way to forgiveness. 'He that covereth his transgressions shall not prosper: But whoso confesseth and forsaketh them shall obtain mercy' (Prov 28¹³). So our psalmist sees that the happiness of the forgiven spirit comes to him in whom there is no deceit. 'Not until man ceases to hide his sin will it be hidden from God' (Kirkpatrick).

But neither his sense of the gravity of sin, nor his understanding of confession, show the greatness of this psalmist. 'Ah, the happiness . . .' He knows the wonder of forgiveness. '*And* thou *forgavest*'—Thou, the God I had fled! This is indeed to be surprised by joy. There is something unchristian in rising from confession still in the gloom of penitence and with the sin still clinging to us. That is to be obsessed by sin. But to take the sin to God and receive His forgiveness, to set out on the new way in the power of His grace, this is to live in the sunshine of religion and the marvel of God's love. 'If we say that we have no sin, we deceive ourselves, and the truth is not in us. If we confess our sins, he is faithful and righteous to forgive us our sins, and to cleanse us from all unrighteousness' (1 Jn 1⁸⁻⁹). And a psalm which began with beatitude ends with a shout of joy:

> '*Be glad in the Lord, and rejoice, ye righteous:*
> *And shout for joy, all ye that are upright in heart.*'

33. Sing Praise to God

After a call to worship, this hymn of praise describes the sovereignty of Yahweh in nature and history, and concludes with an expression of trust in Him.

33[7]. '*as an heap*'. Better 'as in a bottle' (wineskin, as *RSV* and the ancient versions). These are the 'waters which were above the firmament' which give the rain.

True worship consists of gazing on God with rapt adoration, remembering all He is and all He has done.

(1) Faithfulness and unwavering love are the marks of His character. The fullness of the earth is His glory (Isa 6[3]), but the earth is itself filled with His constant love. Because He loves righteousness, pure religion consists not only of a numinous sense of God's ineffable majesty, but also of visiting the fatherless and widows in their affliction and imitating that righteousness of Yahweh which goes beyond bare justice to care for those in distress (cf. Isa 1[11–17], Jas 1[27]).

(2) He is the mighty Creator. The word of God reminds us of the creation story in *Genesis*. The mythologies of the other peoples of the ancient world told of gods who were themselves part of nature, and of creation as the result of strife and death among them. Yahweh is beyond the physical universe, the omnipotent Creator, who has only to speak a word and worlds come into being. This conception of creation may have to be modified by modern knowledge, but it does not have to be discarded. The Christian remembers that to create a world God spoke a word, to save that world He sent *the Word*.

(3) He is active in history. The Israelite could not conceive an absentee God who left men to conduct their own affairs. Yahweh works through history and controls the nations. The fourth beatitude of the Psalter is here—Ah, the happiness of the people whom Yahweh has chosen. Exodus 19[4–6], Deuteronomy 7[6–11], Amos 3[1–2] and 1 Peter 2[9] show the wonderful privilege and the dread responsibility of being the people of God.

(4) He watches over those who trust in His love. The psalmist thinks of safety from death and famine, themes seen in other psalms which may have been sung at the autumn festival. The writer of *Job* teaches that God's providence cannot be understood as simply as this, and a faith which has a cross at its centre sees God's love in the midst of suffering and salvation achieved through pain and loss.

Thus the people praise Yahweh with a '*new song*' (verse 3, cf. 96[1], 98[1]). This is hardly a reference to the present psalm as newly composed for the occasion. It is timelessly new, for it sings the praises of the eternal God. But a *'new song'* also looks forward to the age when Yahweh works the 'new things' of His salvation (see Isa 42¹⁰). The Christian's 'new song' is the worship of the Lamb by the redeemed (see Rev 5⁹).

34. Thanksgiving for Deliverance and Instruction in True Religion

A man who has been saved from his trouble offers his glad thanksgiving to Yahweh and invites his fellow Israelites to join him in his praises and in his experience of God's goodness (verses 1–10). Then, like a teacher of wisdom, he gives instruction in the nature of true religion and tells how Yahweh watches over those who serve Him (verses 11–22). The psalm is another acrostic (cf. 37).

34⁵. The verbs should probably be imperatives (as *RSV* and many of the ancient versions).

34⁷. *'The angel of the Lord'*. The mysterious messenger of Yahweh, who represents Him so completely that he becomes indistinguishable from Yahweh Himself. Here the angel is apparently thought of as a whole army (cf. Gen 16⁷⁻¹⁴, 32¹⁻², Isa 63⁹).

34¹⁷. *'The righteous'* is inserted from several of the ancient versions, but it spoils the metre. It is probable that verses 15 and 16 should be reversed, when 17 will follow naturally on 15. This order of the alphabet is also found in Lamentations 2–4.

It is easy to value this psalm lightly and to treat its teaching as a superficial doctrine of retribution which fails to see the inadequacies of such a belief. This is to miss its true character. It is the thanksgiving of one whom Yahweh has saved from his distress. Although the psalmist refers but briefly to his sufferings (verses 4 and 6), all he says springs from that experience. This is no traditional teaching, no abstract theory. As A. J. Gossip could speak comfort to those whose lives had tumbled in because bereavement had shattered his own life, so this psalmist can speak with the authority of one who has passed the way he teaches. He has a right to speak because he knows. When his heart was broken and bleeding he found God near. When fears and troubles fell upon him he discovered that Yahweh saves. It may be that he does not pierce as deeply into the dark mystery of suffering as Job did. Perhaps his faith was never so shaken that he had to come to God along the unlit tunnel of doubt, as did the writer of 73. But his words are not to be despised because his faith was more serene.

Moreover, his teaching on God's loving care of those who trust Him is far from any doctrine of material rewards or immediate pleasure. He does claim that those who seek Yahweh will not lack any good thing, and this is set in bold contrast to the fate of the wicked (verses 9–10, 16, 20–21). His leading thought, however, is that God comes to help the man who trusts Him when troubles come upon him (verses 4, 6, 17–19), while the primary blessing is to know that Yahweh is by his side, not any safety He may give (verses 8, 15, 18). He has found that, when men's hearts break for sorrow and their spirits are crushed, He who dwells in eternity draws near (see Isa 57^{15}, 61^1, Lk 4^{16-21}).

The psalmist comes to Yahweh with joyful thanksgiving. The psalm taken as a whole reveals his desire to praise God, as the General Thanksgiving has it, 'not only with our lips, but in our lives; by giving up ourselves to Thy service, and by walking before Thee in holiness and righteousness all our days'. Worship is matched by obedience, praise by instruction in the good life.

'The fear of the Lord', a frequent theme in the wisdom writings (see Job 28^{28}, Prov 1^7, 8^{13}, 9^{10}), is that reverent piety which walks humbly with God and is obedient to His will. In this psalm truthful speech (cf. Jas 1^{26}, 3^{2-12}), avoidance of evil, and active goodness are specially mentioned. The quest for peace goes beyond a mere avoidance of strife. Peace has to be 'pursued', energetically sought—it is the peace-*makers* who receive the benediction (Mt 5^9; cf. Rom 14^{19}, 2 Cor 13^{11}, Heb 12^{14}). And since '*peace*' is the fullness of blessing (see on 29^{11}), the psalmist may be calling the godly to that concern for the welfare of others which is not far from the Christian ideal of love of one's neighbour.

This psalmist is an evangelist who calls on others to discover the riches of the religious life. Not fear of disaster but the wonder of life with God is the motive of his plea. 'Ah, the happiness of the man who trusts in Yahweh.' The true urgency of the gospel is here—not the threat of hell or an overhanging temporal distress, but a deep sense of the blessing missed by those who will not come to God. And the psalmist's message is no stern call to live the upright life. Having tasted the goodness of Yahweh, he urges others to come to Him and expects that their response to His kindness will be the glad obedience of gratitude which is the heart of true religion.

35. A Prayer for Vindication in the face of Hostile Accusers

Almost the whole of this psalm is taken up with prayers for the psalmist's deliverance and for the discomfiture of his enemies. This would be natural in the prayer of one who has been falsely accused and now commits his cause to the decision of Yahweh (see 7). It may be that he is sick and his illness is interpreted by his enemies as the punishment of God (see 6 and Job 22⁵⁻¹¹).

35³. '*and stop the way*'. Probably the word is a noun indicating some weapon, perhaps a double-headed war axe (cf. *RV*m).

35¹³ᶜ. The interpretation is doubtful. It is very unlikely that the bowing of the head in prayer is intended (as *RSV*). Probably the sense is similar to Matthew 10¹²⁻¹³, perhaps with the additional idea that the prayer will be effective for himself now that he is in a similar plight.

35¹⁴ᵃ. A change of vowels would give the meaning, 'bowing down (in grief) as for a brother of mine'.

35¹⁵. '*the abjects*'. Different vowels give, 'smiters'—perhaps, 'smiting me unawares' is meant.

35¹⁶ᵃ. The Hebrew appears to mean, 'like the profanest of mockers of a cake' (*RSV*m)! Probably we should change to, 'They impiously mocked more and more' (as *RSV*), or 'as an impious man they mocked me'.

If this is the prayer of one who comes to the sanctuary to receive Yahweh's vindication of his innocence, the apparently vindictive words against his enemies are somewhat softened. Acquittal inevitably means that his accusers are shown to be in the wrong.

Yet special circumstances seem to have increased his bitterness. Those who testify against him are '*malicious witnesses*' (verse 11, *RV*m) who show base ingratitude to one who had been their friend. When they were ill, far from condemning them he had entered into their suffering, grieving for them as if they had been his nearest kin and praying earnestly for them. This is true sympathy, no easy word of commiseration that is forgotten almost as soon as it is spoken, no casual prayer, but a compassion which stood where they were and prayed the prayer which their pain prevented them from uttering. And their recompense is to accuse him when suffering comes upon him, and, instead of seeking his welfare, to mock and look for his ruin! It is small wonder that the psalmist turns on them as Jeremiah did against his persecutors (Jer 18¹⁹⁻²³).

This is not the full Christian way, but before we condemn we should remember how natural it is and how often we adopt the same attitude though we express it less openly. To persist in love of those who spurn the help that is offered and repay friendship with hostility is the height of discipleship that comes only from nearness to Him who knew Himself to be hated without cause (see Jn 15²⁵).

Three times the psalmist takes up his plea and three times, having uttered his complaint and appealed for help, he turns to praise (verses 9–10, 18, 27–8). As in other of these laments the psalmist vows that he will express his thanksgiving in the temple, publicly testifying to Yahweh's goodness, and he calls on those who desire to see him vindicated to join in his gladness. The enemies are now forgotten. All thought is fixed on Yahweh. He delights in the welfare of His servant. He saves the weak and needy. He has spoken to him in truth, '*I am thy salvation*' (verse 3).

36. The Sin of the Wicked and the Goodness of God

The contrast between the description of the sinfulness of the wicked (verses 1–4) and the hymn of praise to Yahweh's goodness (verses 5–9) has suggested to some that two originally separate poems have been joined together. However, the wicked are found again at the end of the psalm, and the

writer probably intended to set the life of the godless over
against the rich blessing of life with God.

36¹⁻². These verses present great difficulties and are almost
certainly corrupt. Two possible interpretations may be suggested.

(*a*) The picture may be that rebellion, personified, speaks to
the wicked man as Yahweh spoke to the prophets. The message
it imparts is probably that there is no need to go in dread of
God, for He pays no heed to sin.

(*b*) If this idea of rebellion's oracle seems too outlandish,
a small alteration would make both verses a description of the
wicked man. 'Rebellion is delightful to the wicked within
his heart' (*AT*). He has no fear of God and deceives himself
into thinking that his sin will not be discovered and punished.

In four verses the character of the wicked man is portrayed.
Instead of eagerly listening to the word of God, he welcomes
the whisper of rebellion. Not even the terror of divine majesty
which drives men into hiding (see Is 2¹⁰, ¹⁹, ²¹) can make him
hesitate, for like the wicked in **10** and **14** he lives as if there
were no God. His words are false and treacherous. He no
longer sets his mind on goodness, but in the quiet of the night,
when men remember God and examine their hearts (4⁴, 63⁶),
he works out his wicked plans. Having deliberately chosen
evil, he no longer shrinks from it with loathing. Were it not
for the dark pages of human story, where men are recorded
whose 'lack of moral sense is so absolute that the occasional
swerve towards decent conduct seems always the effect of
chance, never of grace', this picture would seem exaggerated.
Paul uses words from this psalm to show the depths to which
fallen man can sink—and from which the grace of God can
raise him (Rom 3¹⁸).

For beside the sin of man stands the love of God, love that
is firm and constant and whose height and depth only the
saints know (cf. Eph 3¹⁷⁻¹⁹). The psalmist plunges into
mythology in order to give some hint of the immensity of
Yahweh's goodness. The mountains of God and the cosmic
sea are the measure of His justice; His righteousness which is
always active to save. And in the sanctuary His worshippers
feast on the pleasures of His love. It may be that this psalmist
is here looking beyond the narrow confines of Judaism and

has the vision of God's love reaching out to all mankind, for he replaces Yahweh by '*God*' and speaks of the 'sons of men' finding in Him a Protector and bountiful Host (cf. Isa 56[7]). Life, light, a river of delight and the fountain of life—the Christian finds these in their fullness in Jesus (see Jn 1[4], 4[10, 14]).

From praise the psalmist turns to prayer. He asks that God will maintain His unswerving love to those who are intimate with Him and by their loving obedience show that they know Him, and that He will protect them from the wicked that they be not driven out as refugees or displaced persons. The psalm ends with the certainty that evil is overthrown, a confidence which perhaps springs from some sign given in the temple.

37. Commit Thy Ways to the Lord

This wisdom poem of quiet confidence in God was the inspiration of Paulus Gerhardt's hymn, translated by John Wesley as, 'Commit thou all thy griefs and ways into His hands' (*MHB* 507). It has been called 'a mirror of providence' and 'an antidote to murmuring'.

The psalm is an acrostic. The verses are in pairs and the first word of each pair begins with a different letter through the whole Hebrew alphabet. It has been suggested that this rather artificial structure was used as an aid to the memory. More probably it was thought of as expressing completeness, the total expression of a theme, this psalm being the 'A to Z', as it were, of trust in God.

37[8b]. A change of vowels has been suggested, giving the meaning, 'Fret not thyself to thine own hurt', i.e. fretting recoils on one's own head.

37[20]. '*as the excellency of the pastures*'. The wicked will be as shortlived as the grass and flowers of Palestine. A small change would give, 'as in the burning of ovens'.

37[28c]. This should begin with the next letter of the alphabet and the Greek version supplies the necessary word. Thus we should probably read, 'The unrighteous are driven forth for ever'.

37[35b]. The meaning of the Hebrew is doubtful. The Greek has, 'and exalting himself like the cedars of Lebanon'.

37[36]. '*But one passed by*'. Better, 'And I passed by', with several ancient versions.

Although some try to divide this psalm into sections, each having a dominant idea, there is little development of the thought and it is better to see it as a set of variations on the theme of trust in God. The writer is an old man who from his long experience sets out to teach the young who, he fears, may be driven to that envious discontent which makes faith falter, when they see the wicked apparently prosperous and happy. That this is a real danger can be seen from **73**, where a man of deep spirituality confesses that his trust in God had almost failed as he looked upon the lives of evil men.

It is sometimes said that the doctrine of retribution expounded in this psalm is no different from that of Job's friends, and many feel that the teaching of the psalmist is too facile. He is accused of closing his eyes to much of the tragedy of human existence. Some even suggest that his dogmatic assertions and the constant reiteration of his theme betoken a faith which is none too sure of itself. Before considering these criticisms it is best to set out his teaching.

(1) He warns against envy of the prosperity of the wicked or righteous indignation at their sinfulness, since this may lead to a discontent which doubts God's loving care and ends by abandoning its own integrity (verse 8; cf. 73^{2-14}).

(2) He is certain that the good prosper and the wicked will soon suffer disaster. At times he expresses this rather unguardedly, as if exact rewards are always meted out (see verses 3–4, 11, 18–19, 25–6). Elsewhere, however, he recognizes that things do not work out as neatly as this, yet he asserts that seeming injustice is only temporary. Evil-doing contains its own nemesis within it (verses 14–15), and, although the wicked may have success for a time, punishment will soon come (verses 2, 10, 12–13, 20, 35–6).

(3) This confidence is the outcome of faith that God is active in His world. He watches over those who trust Him, raising them up when they fall, rescuing them from the wicked, and proclaiming their innocence when they are falsely accused (verses 5–6, 17, 24, 28, 33, 39–40).

(4) In spite of his frequent promises of prosperity and material welfare for the righteous, he knows that goodness is valuable in itself, even if it brings no tangible rewards (verse 16). His ideal of goodness is lofty. It is to have God's law in one's heart (verse 31), to wait eagerly for Him and keep His way (verses 7, 9, 34), and to act graciously to those in trouble (verse 21).

(5) His aim is practical. He urges his hearers to commit themselves to God and discover the same serene faith which he possesses (verses 3–5, 7, 27, 34).

The main criticism of this psalmist is that his vision is too narrow. He has only the brief space of man's earthly life in which to justify God's ways with men and he tries to achieve this by gazing at only a part of life. As far as he sees his message is broadly true, and it must not be overlooked that he would never fall into the blasphemy of saying, 'Love God in order to secure earthly happiness'. He has a strong faith in God's righteousness and knows the blessing of a life that is wholly devoted to Him. Had his view been wide enough to comprehend eternity, he might well have attained to the faith which knows that 'right is right, since God is God, and right the day must win', because it possesses the 'instinct that can tell that God is on the field when He is most invisible'. It was the coming of Christ which gave men the sure confidence to risk losing with God in place of the faith that they were certain of winning with Him.

38. Sickness, Loneliness, Guilt

This psalmist is severely ill and has been deserted by his friends and threatened by enemies; conscious of his sin, he prays urgently to God for help.

38[8b]. Perhaps the meaning is, 'I groaned by reason of the yearning of my heart'.

38[9]. '*desire*'. The word may mean 'lament'.

38[17a]. 'I am likely to stumble'.

38[19]. '*are lively*'. A small change would give 'without cause' (cf. verse 19b).

The sufferings of this psalmist are similar to those of Job. Stricken by disease which he regards as the fierce onslaught of an angry God (cf. Job 6[4], 7[20], 16[9, 12-14]), he can find no comfort from men. His friends turn away from him and even his near kinsmen stand afar off, unwilling to associate with one so clearly marked out as a sinner (cf. Job 19[13-19]). Those less friendly mutter their insinuations and watch for his final destruction, although they have no cause to display such cruel enmity (cf. Job 16[10-11], 30[9-15]). But unlike Job who denies that he has committed any sin which merits so great a punishment, the psalmist openly confesses his sin. Perhaps it was only his sickness which first turned his mind to the wrong he had committed, but now that he recognizes it he expresses deep and sorrowful contrition, making no attempt to defend himself against the accusations which are hurled against him by his enemies.

Like the writer of **6**, this psalmist holds the common OT view which linked misfortune inseparably with moral wrongdoing. We are less ready to admit that punishment follows the act of sin in this way, though the psalmist nowhere asserts that the suffering of others is always a proof of their sin. Often, indeed, a man may know in his heart that he deserves the misfortune which has befallen him. His reaction to his troubles, nevertheless, can instruct the Christian. Ill, lonely, conscious of his sin, he turns to God. 'For thee, O Lord, do I wait; It is thou, O Lord my God, who wilt answer' (verse 15, *RSV*). In spite of the punishment which he thinks comes from God, in spite of his sin, he appeals to the One whom he can still call '*my God*', for there is no-one else to whom he can turn for relief.

This is not the greatest of the seven penitential psalms of Christian tradition, yet it holds within it a large part of the secret of true repentance. As Paul knew, there is a regret for a wrong done which only impoverishes the soul. The pain caused us by our sin, our injured pride, our loss of self-respect are our chief thought. We are sorry only because our sin has been found out. There is no cleansing, no strengthening of resolve, no eager longing for holiness, and the experience brings us no closer to God. But there is a 'godly sorrow', 'the pain which God is allowed to guide', that repentance which recognizes its sin, abhors it and disowns it, and through it all turns towards God, not away from Him (see verses 18 and 21-2, and cf. 2 Cor 7[9-10]).

39. 'I am thy passing guest'

A man so ill that death seems near prays to God with a faith
that wrestles with hopelessness.

39[11]. *'like a moth'*. There seem to be three Hebrew words
having an identical form. The meaning here may be that
Yahweh's chastisement destroys a man's bodily strength and
beauty, as a moth devours clothes; but perhaps the sense is
that man's beauty vanishes 'like a bird's-nest' (cf. Job 4[19], 27[18],
where the same word is used to express transitoriness), or
'Thou dissolvest my beauty into festering wounds' (cf. Hos 5[12],
where 'moth' should be 'pus').

The pathos and the glory of this psalm will be missed if the
basic outlook of the writer is not grasped. Like many of the
psalmists, he believes that sickness is God's punishment for
sin, and he has no hope of any life beyond the grave. Although
the psalm has similarities with others, notably **73** and **90**, it
is unique in revealing the spiritual struggles of a man faced
with a seemingly fatal disease. Inconsistencies of thought
and rapid changes of mood reveal the writhings of despera-
tion, and it is wrong to remove them by rearrangements or
emendations.

At first he tries to keep silent, unwilling to voice his questionings where the wicked would seize upon them and where his
apparent impiety could harm the faith of others. He had hoped
that God would heed his silence, but this has not happened.
Now he can keep back his words no longer, but it is to God
and not to men that he addresses them. Even here we see
faith, the faith that can turn to an angry God and pour out
its doubts to Him.

Even as he asks about the meaning of life his thoughts rush
on. How transient and futile it is. A few brief years slip
hurriedly away. Even the rich cannot retain the wealth they
have so anxiously amassed (cf. Lk 12[16-21]). He arrives at a
pessimism very like that of *Ecclesiastes* (verses 1–6).

Quickly, however, he recoils, shrinking back from the abyss
of a meaningless and purposeless existence. His hope is in
God. Suddenly he asks forgiveness for his sin and prays that
the disease which he sees as divine punishment may be healed.
Even while he prays he turns back to gaze at the senselessness

of it all. Man's life is brief enough, a mere breath, yet his own
life is being cut shorter still (verses 7–11).

But again he looks back to Yahweh and a new thought
enters his mind and gives him hope for a moment. His life on
earth, short and fleeting as it is, is like that of the alien who
has settled in Israel, who is wholly dependent on the goodwill
of those among whom he lives since he possesses no rights of
his own. The 'sojourner' had always been accorded special
consideration in the Jewish law (see Ex 22²¹, 23⁹, Lev 19³³⁻⁴,
Deut 10¹⁸⁻¹⁹). He realizes that he possesses guest rights at the
hand of God. Thus he can pray that bright happiness may be
his before he passes to the annihilation of death. Yet even
this prayer contains its own peculiar twist. Other psalmists
ask for Yahweh to turn His face towards them in their need.
He, like Job, flinches from God's anger and prays that He will
look away from him and trouble him no more (verses 12–13;
note *RV*m, and see Job 7¹⁹⁻²⁰, 14¹⁻¹²).

The constant flux of things deeply disturbed the Greeks,
and their main desire was for a salvation that would give
permanence and changelessness. The Israelite had a deeper
awareness of sin and of the wonder of personal fellowship
with the living God. It is only the rare sensitive spirit who
feels the pointlessness of a life that is bounded by the silence
of Sheol. Job expresses poignant longings—if only God would
hide him in Sheol till His anger had passed and then restore
him. This psalmist does not even dare to hope. To the Christian this very darkness lights up the new way in Christ. We
may be sojourners on earth, but we are a colony of heaven
and it is there that our true citizenship belongs (Phil 3²⁰).
Here we may have no abiding city, but we look to the city
which is to come, knowing that this earth is not our home
(see Heb 11⁹⁻¹⁰, ¹³⁻¹⁶, 13¹⁴, and cf. *MHB* 610, 627).

40. Joyful Thanksgiving and a Cry for Help

This psalm falls into two distinct parts. Verses 1–11 are the
thanksgiving of a man who has recovered from a serious illness. The rest of the psalm (and verses 13–17 recur as **70**)
contains a prayer for help against enemies. The marked
differences of form, content and general tone make it likely
that two separate psalms have been joined together.

40⁵. Read as *RV*m.

40⁶⁻⁸. These verses are difficult and perhaps have suffered in transmission. The general sense seems to be that Yahweh does not require sacrifice but rather obedience—teaching that is found in a few other psalms and in the prophets (see 50⁷⁻¹⁵, 51¹⁶⁻¹⁷, 69³⁰⁻¹, 1 Sam 15²², Jer 7²¹⁻³, Hos 6⁶, Mic 6⁶⁻⁸). Some would make this clearer by reading, with a change of vowels, 'If Thou didst delight in . . . Thou wouldst have opened my ears, if Thou didst require . . .', but this is unnecessary.

'*Mine ears hast thou opened*'. Cf. *RV*m. Yahweh has given him the ability to know His will. Heb 10⁵ quotes this from the Greek version, which had an internal corruption in its text, and this suggested the incarnation to the writer of that epistle.

'*In the roll of the book it is written of me*'. The psalmist's obedience is inscribed in a heavenly record (cf Ex 32³², Lk 10²⁰, Rev 3⁵). But the meaning may be, 'it is written *for* me'—Yahweh's requirements are recorded in a written law.

40¹¹. This is probably not a prayer, but a confident assertion —'Thou wilt not withhold . . . Thy lovingkindness and thy truth will continually preserve me.'

(a) Verses 1–11

Without any introduction, the writer plunges immediately into an account of his experience. He has been ill and Yahweh has heard his prayer and healed him. Thinking of sickness as a form of death, he pictures his recovery as a deliverance from Sheol itself (cf. 30³, 69¹⁻², ¹⁴⁻¹⁵, 88³⁻⁶, and Jonah 2²⁻⁹, another individual thanksgiving). Now he has come to the temple to express his thanksgiving in a song of praise. Normally such a worshipper would offer a sacrifice, but this psalmist believes that men's gratitude is best expressed by eager obedience.

Having received such great blessing, he cannot avoid becoming an evangelist. 'I have told the glad news of deliverance in the great congregation' (verse 9, *RSV*). He piles up words to describe Yahweh's salvation—righteousness, faithfulness, lovingkindness, truth. Great is the happiness of the man who makes Yahweh his ground of trust (verse 4). Nor can he remain a solitary. He links his own deliverance with all the occasions when Yahweh has come to the help of His people (verse 5). Thus he can end his psalm in the confidence that Yahweh will always support him with His changeless love.

In spite of the use of part of this psalm by the writer to the Hebrews, who quotes it to prove the superiority of the willing and obedient sacrifice of Jesus over the animal sacrifices of the Jewish law, it is best viewed as a perfect example of thanksgiving. The self is utterly effaced. Even the distress from which the psalmist was delivered is lightly touched upon. His whole gaze is directed onto God's ineffable goodness. His wonderful works are beyond man's telling. How then can a man show his thankfulness? Even his hymns of praise have been given him by God. Sacrifice cannot express his gratitude. The only possible response is joyful obedience. And with this obedience goes the desire to tell others, for he cannot hide God's saving help within his heart. The salvation which leads him to thanksgiving must lead others to awe and trust.

(b) Verses 12–17

Little need be said about this short lament. The theme is found in several other psalms and many of the phrases occur elsewhere in the Psalter.

41. True and False Sympathy

As he expresses his thanksgiving for renewed health, the psalmist recalls his prayer when he was ill, and remembers with some bitterness the hostility of his enemies and the betrayal of his nearest friend.

41³. '*Thou makest all his bed in his sickness*'. The meaning is probably that Yahweh turns his sickness to health, rather than that He rearranges his bed to ease his pain, though the expression is a little odd; some emend (cf. *RSV*).

41¹⁰. '*that I may requite them*'. Perhaps this is not as vindictive as it sounds. The psalmist may only mean that his recovery will disprove the evil prophecies of his enemies (cf. 13⁴, 40¹⁴⁻¹⁵).

Although this seems to be a thanksgiving (see verses 11–12), most of the psalm consists of a lament, while the first three verses are similar to wisdom teaching and describe the blessing which comes to those who are considerate towards the help-less. It is just possible that the whole psalm is a lament, and that the confidence expressed at the end is that certainty that Yahweh has heard the prayer which is found in other laments.

The prayer for healing and help against the enemies is much like that of other psalms (e.g. **6, 13, 31**), but the hostility of the enemies is described in full detail. They watch for his death. With hypocritical kindness they visit him, but only that they may gloat over his sufferings. 'A friendly face masks a cold heart.' It is even possible that they have been dabbling in sorcery and now are waiting for their curses to have their effect. His most trusted friend, who was bound to him by the closest ties of friendship that had been sealed by the sharing of a meal, has turned against him (verse 9, applied in Jn 13[18] to Judas).

The psalm shows up the failure of much of our sympathy. Few there are who can offer real friendship, who are genuinely cut to the heart when others go wrong or feel as if the trouble had come crashing into their own lives when others are over-taken by misfortune. The whispered, 'Have you heard about...?' reveals a spirit into which love has scarcely found an entrance.

By contrast, the beatitude with which this psalm opens digs deep into the meaning of truly caring. Understanding, tact, and the intuition which knows when to offer help and when to stand aside are all there. One of the special marks of OT piety is the giving of help to those who have no wealth to sus-tain them, no rights on which to rely, no-one to give support in difficult times (see **72**[2, 4, 12–14], Job 29[12–17], 30[25], 31[16–22]).

The final verse of the psalm is probably a doxology set at the end of the first book of the Psalter.

42–3. 'As pants the hart for cooling streams'

The refrain in **42**[5, 11] and **43**[5], together with similarities of language and thought, show that this is really one psalm. There are three stanzas, each ending with the refrain.

An exile who can no longer worship in the temple, and is probably also ill, pleads urgently for God's help.

42[2]. '*appear before God*'. Rather 'behold the face of God' (as *RSV*). The traditional reading is almost certainly a

deliberate alteration by the Jewish scribes out of reverence for
Yahweh.

42^{4b}. The text is difficult. Some, partly following the Greek
version, read, 'How I went unto the tent of the Glorious One,
unto the house of God'.

42^{5}. The refrain should be altered to the form in **42^{11}, 43^{5}.**

42^{6}. Probably this is where the psalmist is now forced to live,
in the far north of Palestine near where the town of Caesarea
Philippi was later built.

42^{7}. This seems to be a description of his sickness as of the
powers of chaos overwhelming him (cf. **18^{4}, 69$^{1-2, 14-15}$,**
Jonah 2^{3}), rather than a picture of the rushing torrents and
waterfalls of the country near the source of the Jordan.

Two things stand out in this psalm; the psalmist's deep
yearning for God, and the importance of the temple worship
in his religious life. Although he pleads for vindication and
deliverance from his enemies, and passionately desires to
return to the temple, his real longing is for God Himself.
He is like a hind which rushes panting from one dried up
watercourse to another, looking for water in a time of drought
(see Jer 14$^{2-6}$ for a vivid picture of drought in Palestine).
The phrases he uses of Yahweh reveal his intense devotion.
He thirsts for the living God, the God of his life, whose
activity is in strong contrast to the gods of the heathen, and
who gives 'life' in all its fullness to His worshippers (**42$^{2, 8}$**).
He is a rock and stronghold (**42^{9}, 43^{2}**) and 'the gladness of my
joy' (**43^{4},** *RV*m).

His personal life is linked with the congregational worship.
He sustains his faith with memories of the times when he
joined with others in the pilgrim feasts in the temple. Then
all was joy and praise. With heartfelt longing he cries out,
Oh that God would send His light and truth as emissaries to
bring me back to the temple where I can once again see God's
face (**42$^{2, 4}$, 43$^{3-4}$**). At a time when many complain that
services are dull, boring and meaningless we look with some
surprise at this psalmist. To him the temple worship is no

bare external ritual, no tedious and wearying duty. It is a moment of gladness and spiritual exaltation, the foundation of his intensely personal religion.

But now he is cut off from this worship. Those who do not share his faith and cannot understand his longing to go to the temple stand mocking. '*Where is thy God?*' ($42^{3,\ 10}$). He feels utterly bereft. His burning desire for God meets no response. Why has God forgotten him? Why this crushing sorrow and heartless taunting? Why does no help come? (42^{9}, 43^{2}). His reply to these questionings is to search his own heart. He knows God. He is his salvation and his God. The assurance of a deep faith enables him to wait for Him in confident hope.

44. 'Deliver us for the sake of thy steadfast love!'

The setting of this communal lament can be seen in 2 Chronicles 20. Israel has been defeated in battle. The people come to the temple in great distress, unable to understand why God has not given them victory, and beseeching Him to help them.

44^{2}. '*and didst spread them abroad*'. This refers to Israel and has a parallel meaning to 'and plantedst them in'. To read, 'and causedst them to put forth shoots' would make this clearer. Israel is described as a vine sending out shoots (cf. 80^{8-11}).

44^{4}. The first letter of the verb '*command*' in the Hebrew has been wrongly attached to the previous word. This is not a petition and we should read, '*my* God, who commandest', as *RSV*.

The people begin their lament almost with a hymn. They recall the traditions handed down from the distant past, which told of the way God brought His people into Canaan and gave them the land after driving out their enemies. These stories were passed on from father to son and recited at the great festivals (see Ex 10^{2}, 12^{26-7}, Deut 6^{20-5}, Josh $4^{6-7,\ 21-4}$). The activity of God was emphasized and the struggles and failures forgotten, for this was a holy war which Yahweh Himself was waging for Israel, because He loved them (cf. Deut 4^{37-8},

7⁷⁻⁸, 9⁴⁻⁶). This is the mighty saving God to whom they now
address their prayer (verses 1–3).

It is easy to look back to the past and regard it as the age of
faith, when the grace of God was active among His people and
new levels of goodness were attained, martyrs died with
courage and joy, and the Church was triumphant. Certainly
Christianity brought a great flood of godliness into a tired and
often vicious world, and there is little to be praised in that
clever superiority which delights in debunking the saints. It is
doubtful, however, whether our struggles towards a firmer
faith are advanced by overlooking the fightings and the fears
that were present in that golden age of our nostalgic longings.
The important thing is God's '*favour*', that love which cannot
be earned by good deeds and does not depend on any merit or
attractiveness of ours; which remains firm even where it wins
no response and never ceases to care however often it is met
by folly or sin.

Remembering that it was God alone who gave victory to
His people and not their own strength, they reaffirm their confidence in Him (verses 4–8).

Then comes the lament. God has allowed His people to be
defeated. Some have been taken prisoner. Neighbouring
nations scoff at their humiliation (verses 9–16).

In verses 17–22 the Israelites state emphatically, that they
have committed no sin which might have explained this
reverse. They have not violated the covenant. God who knows
all must see that they have been true to Him. It is wrong to
condemn this as the self-righteousness which stubbornly
refuses to acknowledge any sin in itself. The claim is more
limited. The people assert that they have been guilty of no
apostasy such as should have brought this disaster.

This leads to renewed and violent petition. As if God were
asleep, they try to wake Him. Their urgent request is based
on the steadfast love of God, by which He remains faithful to
His covenant (verses 23–6).

To a Christian who does not regard the Father of Jesus as
a God of armies this psalm may seem to belong entirely to
the Old Covenant. Some, indeed, have shuddered at the
irreverence which sarcastically speaks of God as a slave owner
who has made a bad bargain in selling His own people, and
which even dares to say, '*Awake, why sleepest thou, O Lord*?'
rather as Elijah mocked the priests of Baal (1 Kings 18²⁷).

Others have seen the psalm as an example of the wrong turning which Judaism took when it failed to see that all is of grace and that man's obedience is his response to the divine initiative of love, not a way of securing God's protection.

Yet we should not overlook the faith in a God who saved Israel because of His free favour, and to whom men can appeal confidently because of His faithfulness and His unwavering love. Even the protestations of innocence show that the people recognize that they must give themselves in utter devotion to Yahweh. This psalm probably comes from an earlier period than the times of the Maccabees when faithful Jews died in their innocence rather than violate God's laws, even though they had not been prepared for persecution as the first Christians had been and while there was no certain hope of a life beyond. Yet the spirit of those martyrs is already seen in verse 22.

But why should this suffering come to those who have been loyal to Yahweh? Why does He not intervene? The psalm reveals a deep perplexity. The puzzle cannot find even the beginnings of a solution until God seemed to hide His face from the devotion of the Son Himself (Mk 15^34). But after that, Paul can quote verse 22 with victory in his heart, for he knows that nothing now can separate us from the love of God (Rom 8^31-9).

45. The King's Wedding

This is a song for a royal wedding. Although it has probably been preserved in the Psalter because it was applied to the messianic king and his bride Israel, it belongs to the marriage of a historical king. Who this king was is quite uncertain. Ahab has been frequently put forward, because the bride in the psalm seemed to be a princess from Tyre. Other suggestions are Solomon, Joram of Judah, and even Aristobulus I. The last of these is extremely unlikely, and there is really no evidence to make any name more than a guess.

The text is not very well preserved and the exact meaning is uncertain in a number of places—see *RSV* for some alternative readings.

45^6. '*Thy throne, O God, is for ever and ever*'. This cannot be an aside addressed to Yahweh, as the Aramaic paraphrase

understood it, but, like the rest of the section, must apply
to the king. According to the *RV*, the king was called *'God'*.
This would be unique in the OT, for although the king occupied
a very exalted position in ancient Israel, and as Yahweh's
anointed and adopted son was His representative, his person
being sacrosanct and inviolable (cf. 2, 1 Sam 26[11], 2 Sam 7),
he is never more than the first among men. This interpretation, therefore, would have to be explained as poetic enthusiasm
perhaps influenced by the court songs from other countries of
the ancient Near East. Some soften the difficulty by assuming
textual corruption and making emendations. If the present
reading is accepted the analogy of, 'Thine eyes are doves' (i.e.
'like those of doves', Song 1[15]) suggests that a literal 'Thy
throne is God, for ever' is to be interpreted as 'Thy throne is
everlasting like that of God'.

45[12]. *'the daughter of Tyre'* may be the people of Tyre (as
RSV), not a princess.

After expressing his eagerness to compose his song (verse 1),
the poet praises the king. He possesses the bodily beauty and
eloquent speech that mark a king. A mighty warrior, may he
be victorious in the cause of righteousness, maintaining true
justice at home. Joy and splendour adorn him (verses 2–9).
Turning to the princess, he urges on her the duty of allegiance
to the king, her new lord, and describes her bridal attire
(verses 10–15). His final wishes are for many descendants and
great renown (verse 16–17).

The strong Israelite emphasis on righteousness and justice
marks this ideal of kingship (see 72). Moreover, the inclusion
of this song in the OT shows that nothing is secular to the
Bible, save sin. Religion enters every part of life. In the same
way the Song of Songs, those love poems whose eroticism was
once held to be beyond the cultivated taste of western readers,
bears witness to the divine acceptance of human love.

The psalm was regarded as a messianic prophecy from early
times. The Aramaic translation paraphrased verse 2 as, 'Thy
beauty, O King Messiah, exceeds that of the children of men;
a spirit of prophecy is bestowed upon thy lips,' while Hebrews
1[8–9] quotes verses 6–7 to show the superiority of Jesus to the
angels. In Christian liturgical tradition it is sung on Christmas
Day. Such interpretations, so far removed from the intention

G

of the author, repel many, striking them as utterly forced and
false. Yet to take this psalm and then to sing,

> *My heart is full of Christ and longs,*
> *Its glorious matter to declare!*
> *Of Him I make my loftier songs,*
> *I cannot from His praise forbear;*
> *My ready tongue makes haste to sing*
> *The glories of my heavenly King* (*MHB* 270).

is not to cling to what is written with a blind determination
which will distort and twist rather than relinquish. Rather
it is to seize upon living symbols to express the light which is
in Christ.

46, 47, 48. Divine Deliverance

These three psalms belong together, having the same themes
and background, **47** being also closely connected with **93,
95–9**. They have been interpreted in three ways.

(*a*) Some think that they are hymns of thanksgiving which
were sung to celebrate the deliverance of Jerusalem from
Sennacherib in 701 B.C. Such a notable example of Yahweh's
saving power might well have called forth the praise of His
people, and reminiscences of the events have been seen in
such passages as **48**$^{4-8}$. The refrain, '*The Lord of hosts is
with us*', in **46** recalls Isaiah's Immanuel prophecy (Isa 7^{14}),
made a few years before, while the stress on the kingship of
God might well be due to the striking way in which His
universal sovereignty had been revealed.

(*b*) Others suggest that the psalms are really prophecies.
Feeling that no known historical events are adequately re-
flected in words which seem more grandiose than the facts
would warrant, even allowing for poetic exaggeration, they
believe that the reference is to God's final victory at the end of
time, when He will achieve full supremacy and bring in an age
of peace, with all the peoples acknowledging Him as Lord
(see **46**$^{8-10}$, **47**$^{6-10}$, **48**^{10}). This would make the psalms similar
to such prophecies as Isaiah 2$^{2-4}$.

(*c*) It seems more probable that the psalms belong to the
temple worship in Jerusalem, and this is the interpretation
adopted here. We have seen in **24** that the ritual probably

included a procession into the temple. Here are three hymns which were sung before and after it.

46. 'A safe stronghold our God is still'

This psalm inspired Luther's famous hymn (*MHB* 494). Three stanzas, each ending with a refrain, proclaim Yahweh as the great Creator who defends His people and establishes His universal rule.

46³. The refrain in verses 7 and 11 seems to have fallen out after this verse.

46⁴ᵇ. Either, 'The holy habitation of the Most High', (as *RSV*), or, partly following the Greek version, 'Which the Most High has sanctified as His abode'. On '*the Most High*' see Genesis 14¹⁸⁻²⁴. This is a title apparently intimately associated with the Jerusalem worship and possibly taken over from the pre-Israelite cultus, but as is shown by the refrain with its expressly Israelite titles for God, the Canaanite worship was transformed when it was taken over (cf. **95**).

46⁹. '*chariots*'. Probably we should change the vowels to read 'shields', with the Greek and Aramaic versions.

The first stanza shows Yahweh powerful over the forces of chaos—the waters of the great deep which provide the life-giving rains and springs, but are ever ready to break out and destroy life. But His people need never fear, even if the primeval destructive void should return, for this mighty God is ready to help in time of trouble. He is both willing and able to save (verses 1-3).

In verses 4-7 Jerusalem, the holy city, is the main theme. The Most High has made it His dwelling-place. At daybreak (see verse 5, *RV*m) He brings help to His people, for like the sun which is perhaps a symbol of His powerful presence, He triumphs over the forces of darkness and scatters the enemies of His chosen nation. The river is probably the river of para-dise which gives fertility and blessing, and which God pro-vided when He created the world. The idea is taken up in the prophets. Isaiah says that, because the men of Judah would not accept in trustful faith the waters of Shiloah, God's waters of blessing, He will allow the rushing flood waters of their enemies to overwhelm them (Isa 8⁶⁻⁸). In Ezekiel's vision of the restored land, a river of life flows from Jerusalem and sweetens even the poisonous waters of the Dead Sea (Ezek 47). In John's New Jerusalem, the river of the water of life proceeds from out of the throne of God and of the Lamb, for it is through Christ that this life comes to men (Rev 22¹, cf. Jn 4¹⁰, 7³⁷).

Finally, the congregation is called on to look at the ritual drama acted before it, in which God's victory over His enemies, destroying bow, spear and shield and establishing universal peace, is vividly portrayed. This is a war to end wars, but unlike men's victories which only breed future conflicts, Yahweh truly brings peace, for His victory is the defeat of evil itself. A prophet then speaks in the name of God. Let the people rest upon Yahweh in quiet confidence. He alone is exalted. Worship is no escape from life. It is an expression of the supreme truth which faith makes real in daily living (verses 8–11).

'*Be still, and know that I am God*'. But modern man is always busy and his rush of doing prevents him remembering God's existence. Meditation is almost a lost art in an age which demands that everything that men do should be 'productive', and as a result the sense of God's nearness is in danger of being lost.

47. 'God has gone up with a shout'

The ark, the symbol of Yahweh's presence, has been carried in procession up to the temple (see **24**). Now all are summoned to praise Him, for He has ascended Mount Zion as a victorious king and reigns triumphant over His enemies.

47⁷. '*with understanding*'. The word is found in the titles of several of the psalms (cf. **32**) where it seems to mean 'a skilful psalm' (unless it had some cultic significance). This may be the meaning here (see *RV*m). It has been suggested that the word has retained its verbal sense, 'Sing the praises of God for His soundness of judgement' ('as One who deals wisely'; cf. Jer 23⁵). The *RV* may be included in our collection of mistranslations. As Paul is quick to point out, praise only wings its way to heaven if it is borne up by the Spirit; yet without an understanding of our faith the most ecstatic devotion cannot sustain the life of the worshipper or build up the Church (see 1 Cor 14).

47⁸. '*God reigneth*'. Either, 'Yahweh is King', expressing His continual sovereignty, or 'Yahweh has become King', with reference to His cultic enthronement.

47⁹. '*shields*'; i.e. rulers.

Yahweh is the great king over the whole earth. He has subdued the nations, the enemies of Israel and those forces hostile to Him, and now sits enthroned and universally acclaimed with loud shouts of praise and the clapping of hands.

This is a special psalm for Ascension Day and forms the basis of Charles Wesley's Ascension hymn, 'God is gone up on high'. As in the cult Yahweh ascended His throne, having asserted His sovereignty once for all, so the ascension of Christ celebrates the triumph of His conquering love. And as the victory of Yahweh over the nations ensures that of Israel, so with our Lord,

> *His foes and ours are one,*
> * Satan, the world, and sin;*
> *But He shall tread them down,*
> * And bring His kingdom in:*
>
> *Till all the earth, renewed*
> * In righteousness divine,*
> *With all the hosts of God*
> * In one great chorus join.*
> *Join all on earth, rejoice and sing;*
> *Glory ascribe to glory's King.'*   (*MHB* 219)

48. 'The city of the great King'

This seems to be a description of the ritual drama before Yahweh entered His temple as a victorious warrior. In this ritual, Yahweh showed His love for His people by defeating their enemies, the kings of the nations and the forces of 'Death'.

48¹. '*in his holy mountain*'. The metre shows that this should be taken with verse 2, as *RSV*.

48². '*on the sides of the north*'. Rather, 'the recesses of the North' (cf. Isa 14¹³, and see below).

48⁷. 'Like an east wind which shatters the ships of Tarshish', Phoenician 'refinery ships' which carried cargo from their refineries in distant Sardinia and Spain, and so deep-sea ships (cf. 1 Kings 10²², Isa 2¹⁶ and our 'East Indiamen').

48⁹. '*We have thought on*'. The verb almost certainly means, 'we have pictured'; an indication that the worshippers were present at a symbolic ritual. This is also brought out in verse 8, where the worshippers say that they have *seen* this victory *within* the city and have been instructed as to its meaning.

48¹⁴. Probably, 'He is our Leader against Death'.

The Canaanite religious texts discovered at Ras Shamra light up this psalm at several points. In those myths, the mountain of the gods where Baal had his throne is described as in the 'recesses of the North'. The exact phrase is used here of Jerusalem. Moreover, a central theme of some of those stories is the conflict between Baal and Mot, or Death. Yet the myths have been transformed. The 'recesses of the North' indicates that Yahweh dwells in no far distant mythical mountain, but in the midst of His people in their very earthly city which is His holy mountain. Yahweh's battle with His enemies contains no suggestion that they are rival gods or that He Himself will die and rise like some fertility deity. Rather they are identified with the national enemies of Israel and all those deathly and enfeebling forces which thwart the full life and welfare of the nation.

Opening with praises to Yahweh as the great King in mount Zion (verses 1–3), the psalm vividly describes the ritual. The hostile kings assembled against Israel, but at the appearance of Yahweh they were dispersed in panic (verses 4–9). Because He has maintained His steadfast love for His people and by His victory has established His righteousness in the world, the men of Judah can rejoice and move in a festal procession through the city, for Yahweh has proved Himself their Leader against 'Death' (verses 10–14).

This is appointed as a proper psalm for Whitsunday, doubtless because the Church was identified with mount Zion. There is grave danger, however, in being 'at ease in Zion'. The psalm shows the way to the true security. In spite of the loving descriptions of the beauty of the city, the stronghold of its inhabitants is Yahweh, the great King, who has made Himself known by His victory over evil.

> *Zion's God is all our own,*
>   *Who on His love rely;*
> *We His pardoning love have known,*
>   *And live to Christ, and die.* (*MHB* 699)

49. Foolish Confidence and True Confidence

A wisdom psalm, akin to 37 and 73, considers the problem of the prosperity of the rich. After an introduction (verses 1–4), in which the psalmist calls on all men to hear his discussion of life's riddle, the psalm falls into two sections, each ending with a refrain (verses 5–12, 13–20). The writer has pondered much upon this problem, and now he has set to music thoughts which came to him as if by direct inspiration.

The text is difficult in several places, and *RV*m and the plausible emendations of *RSV* should be noticed.

49⁵ᵇ. 'when the iniquity of my persecutors surrounds me', as *RSV*.

49⁶. Compare **52⁷**, **62¹⁰**, Job 31²⁴⁻⁵, Ecclus 11¹⁸⁻¹⁹, Mk 10¹⁷⁻²⁷, Lk 6²⁴, 12¹³⁻²¹, 16¹⁹⁻³¹, Jas 5¹⁻⁶. The frequent emphasis in the scriptures on the dangers of riches gives little comfort to those in the West, for we are the rich, at whose gate Lazarus lies, and who have so exalted the bourgeois virtues that envy, avarice and greed are not even recognized as sins. Property tends to be ranked above persons, finance governs most policies, and the comforts of wealth are a sore drag on the spiritual quest.

49⁸. Probably, 'for the ransom of his life is costly', as *RSV*.

49¹². The refrain differs slightly from verse 20. Perhaps this was intentional, but the Greek and Syriac versions read both verses in the form found in verse 20. *RSV* changes verse 20 to agree with this present verse.

49¹⁴. 'Like sheep they are appointed for Sheol;
Death shall be their shepherd;
straight to the grave they descend,
and their form shall waste away;
Sheol shall be their home.' (*RSV*).

The psalmist's questionings arose out of his experience. He has been treated harshly by the rich, who feel secure in their self-confidence in their riches. Probably also he envies them their wealth. His thoughts at first lead him to the realization that, though a rich man can often escape punishment by paying a fine (see Ex 21²⁸⁻³⁰), a limit has been set to this by God. In death a man meets the supreme power of God Himself, and this shows up the foolishness and weakness of his confidence in his wealth. Death, indeed, is the great leveller; wise men and fools, good men and the obstinate and self-willed man and the beasts all find in the grave their only permanent dwelling.

In the second half of the psalm, the writer draws the grotesque picture of death as a shepherd, driving his flock to Sheol, where they will remain to waste away the shadowy end of their existence. Against this life, in which death has the last word, he sets his own, in which the last word is God's; against a foolish confidence in riches he puts his own sure confidence in God.

'God will ransom me from the power of Sheol, He will take me' (verse 15). Some have thought that this is no more than a conviction that God will save him from premature death, and is an expression of his belief that poverty which knows fellowship with God is superior to riches with no sense of His presence. It seems more likely, however, that here we have another leap of faith. Perhaps with a remembrance of the way God took Enoch and Elijah to Himself so that they did not see death (Gen 5²⁴, 2 Kings 2), perhaps with no very clear idea of what the future will be, he is none the less certain that God will save him even from the world of the dead, for God has power over Sheol itself.

The mention of ransom turns the mind of the Christian to the One who came as a servant and gave His life as a ransom for many (Mk 10⁴⁵). What man could never do for himself (see verse 7) God has done for Him in Christ, releasing him from the bondage of sin and the fear of death, and opening up the hope of eternal life in the presence of his Lord. But the ransom was far more costly than the psalmist ever realized.

The writer is a teacher, and he ends his song with an exhortation to the poor not to fear or envy the rich, since they will all die and leave their wealth behind. This may appear a rather meagre consolation, especially after the joyful hope of verse 15. It serves to show that almost all the glances which are cast towards a life of fellowship with God after death in the OT are tentative and faltering. Certainty does not come until Christ is seen raised from the dead (see 1 Cor 15, 2 Tim 1¹⁰, Heb 2¹⁴⁻¹⁵). So confident is Paul that death seems to him the least of the things which can cut a man off from God (Rom 8³⁸). Today, however, we doubt afresh. Indeed, the NT is often unhelpful to us, because it seems to contain so little doubt, so few struggles after faith. The OT psalmist speaks far more closely for us. And we, like him, have to build up our trust painfully and hesitatingly upon our experience of God here and now (see on **16** and **73**). If we were more intimate with Him we should perhaps come nearer to the quiet calm of Richard Baxter:

Lord, it belongs not to my care
  Whether I die or live;
To love and serve Thee is my share,
  And this Thy grace must give. (*MHB* 647. The whole hymn is worth careful study.)

50. Right Worship and True Obedience

This is a prophetic liturgy. An introduction depicts God coming in majesty to judge His people (verses 1–6). He condemns them for their false ideas of worship (verses 7–15) and their failure to match their confession of faith with their way of life (verses 16–21). The psalm ends with a warning and a promise, rather like the blessing and the curse which came at the conclusion of the law (verses 22–3; cf. Deut 28).

It is difficult to decide the setting of this psalm. Many

similarities with the teaching of the prophets have suggested
that it is a didactic poem based on their teaching (e.g. see
the judgement scene in Isa 1², Mic 1²⁻⁴, 6¹⁻²; the teaching
about sacrifice in Isa 1¹⁰⁻¹⁵, Jer 7²¹⁻³, Amos 5²¹⁻⁵, Mic 6⁶⁻⁸;
and the demands for righteousness in Isa 1¹⁶⁻¹⁷, ²¹⁻⁶, Hos
4¹⁻³, Amos 2⁶⁻¹⁶, 5²⁴). But perhaps it comes from a prophet
or priest attached to the temple, who expounded the requirements of the covenant at a festival celebrating its renewal (see
verse 5).

50¹⁸. '*thou consentest with him*'. Much stronger—'thou didst
delight thyself with him', didst gladly associate with him (see
RSV).

50²⁰. '*speakest against*'. Perhaps the meaning is, 'turnest thy
back on'.

50²¹. See Rom 3²⁵. Paul says that the appalling horror of
the Cross was accepted by God expressly that men could never
say again that sin was of no concern to Him.

50²³ᵇ,ᶜ. The Hebrew is difficult and unrhythmical. One suggestion is to alter to, 'To him who walks perfectly I will show
my salvation'.

The coming of Yahweh on Sinai was accompanied by thick
cloud and lightning. God was shrouded by blinding light and
impenetrable darkness (see Ex 19¹⁶⁻¹⁹, Deut 4¹¹, 5²²⁻⁴).
This was how later Israel always imagined His appearing (see
Jud 5⁴⁻⁵, Hab 3³⁻⁶, and the notes on 18⁷⁻¹⁵). So it is in this
psalm. But the setting has changed. Yahweh's splendour
shines forth now from Zion, the city He has chosen in the land
He gave to His people. He is not a God who is far off and to
whom men must make their way by costly pilgrimage, or who
is too distant to concern Himself with how they live (cf.
Jer 23²³⁻⁴).

Heaven and earth are called as witnesses, for His judgement
of Israel is of significance to the whole universe. The dis-
tinctions between right and wrong are no trivialities which a
wider view can overlook. Thus the judgement scene is set, and
it reveals the essence of the accusation. It is as though Yahweh
were asking His people, 'Do you belittle me?' El, God,
Yahweh, the Most High—the titles are massed as if to say,

This is the Mighty One whom you would bring down to the level of your own petty thoughts.

Do you belittle me in your worship?—'I am God, your God' (verse 7, *RSV*). The sacrifices are duly offered, doubtless with careful attention to the correct ritual and their costliness, and the people think that God will be satisfied! As if the Creator of the world needed men's gifts! As if they can buy Him off with presents! The only sacrifice they can offer is thanksgiving (verse 14). It probably goes beyond the psalmist's intention to interpret this in a purely spiritual sense, verbal thanksgiving being a higher substitute for animal sacrifices. He means that the worshippers should recognize that it is the intention of the heart which makes the offering acceptable. And if they understood His true nature aright, they would simply pray to Him in time of trouble, knowing that He delights to save.

Do you belittle me in your daily life? The Israelites claim to be God's covenant people, and recite His commandments and think that this is sufficient to satisfy Him. Without compunction they mix with thieves and adulterers, readily speak ill of others, and are completely lacking in courtesy and consideration to members of the family circle (see Rom 1[32]). And they think that all this does not matter to God, because He has not inflicted an immediate punishment!

What conception of God does our worship and our daily life betray? Is there that sense of rapt amazement that we, the creatures of time and rebels against God, should be able to address the Holy One who inhabits eternity? Or is there that casual nonchalance which regards public worship as a favour bestowed upon God? Do we trade upon God's patience, heedless of the knowledge that His forbearance should lead us back to the Cross (see Rom 2[4]—Paul says that by doing this we, insignificant and sinful creatures of time, 'despise', look down on, God Himself)? Or do we shrink back as we listen once again to the great commandments to love, and tremble in the penitence that is consumed with its burning desire to be perfect as He is perfect, to have that purity of heart which can gaze upon God?

51. 'Create in me a clean heart, O God'

This, the greatest of the psalms of penitence, comes very near to the spirit of the NT, and Christians from early times have

found it an expression of their own sense of sin. The gravity
of sin and the immensity of God's grace stand out clearly.

51⁶. '*in the inward parts*'. In Job 38³⁶, the only other place
where this word occurs, it seems to mean the 'hidden places'
of the heavens. Perhaps the meaning is, 'Thou hast stored up
truth in the hidden places'. God alone can reveal the wisdom
of the perfect way to man.

51¹¹. '*thy holy spirit*'. The phrase is found only here and
Isaiah 63¹⁰⁻¹¹ in the OT. The wonder of grace is that, how-
ever often man grieves God's Spirit, He never withdraws
Himself from him.

51¹⁴. '*blood-guiltiness*'. Normally this means 'deeds of
violence, murder'. Here death as punishment may be intended
(cf. 30⁹). Some would change the vowels to read 'silence', the
silence of Sheol.

51¹⁷. '*The sacrifices of God*'. Probably, 'My sacrifice, O God'
(with a change of vowels).

51¹⁹. '*sacrifices of righteousness*'. Sacrifices offered with the
correct ritual (cf. 4⁵).

Like the writer of **32** (cf. the notes there), this psalmist has a
deep understanding of the true nature of sin.

(*a*) He recognizes that the word sin has no meaning apart
from God. A man may regret that he has fallen short of the
best that he might have been, he may feel bitter remorse over
an injury he has done to his fellow-man, but he does not
repent of his *sin* until he says with David, 'I have sinned
against the Lord' (2 Sam 12¹³; cf. Gen 39⁹). Yet, as Amos saw
so clearly, it is not lapses in religious practice which alone are
sins against God. Oppression, fraud, injustice and the lack of
common humanity are all His concern. Christ made this
insight yet more pointed with His, 'Ye did it not unto me'
(Mt 25⁴⁵; cf. 1 Cor 8¹²).

(*b*) He looks into his heart and sees that he has sinned from
the first and that there is little he can do to change his character. Although verse 5 was influential in the development of
asceticism in the Christian Church, it does not teach that

marriage is sinful. Celibacy has no special virtue in the OT.
Rather, the psalmist is conscious that he is a member of a
sinful race. The environment in which he grew up was saturated with evil, and as he learnt to distinguish between right
and wrong he found that his desire and will were opposed to
God and always he had a propensity towards evil (see Gen 8²¹,
Job 15¹⁴⁻¹⁶, 25⁴, Isa 6⁵, Rom 3²³).

(c) He realizes that the most serious consequence of sin is
not any punishment which is justly deserved nor any blighted
hopes which come in its train. Its worst effect is that it destroys
communion with God. 'Your iniquities have made a separation between you and your God' (Isa 59², *RSV*). To be shut
out from God's presence! The psalmist shudders. It is not
being found out which troubles his soul (verse 11; cf. **27⁹**).

Repentance, however, requires not only a knowledge of sin,
but also a knowledge of grace. This is where the psalmist begins. Be gracious unto me, remember Thy covenant love, forgive according to the abundance of Thy compassion. He relies
upon the character of God. He is confident of God's free
favour, His faithfulness, His fatherly tenderness (cf. Ex 34⁶⁻⁷).
Thus when he comes to God as he must, for only God can
forgive sin, he does not come in fear. And he comes to God
because He alone can enable him to live the good life. The
way to goodness does not lie in trying each day to do better in
the hope of one day doing well. Goodness comes from the
new, pure heart which only God can create (verse 10; the
Hebrew word is used of the creation of the world in Gen 1,
and is used only for God, never of man; for the idea here see
Jer 24⁷, 31³³, Ezek 36²⁵⁻⁷, 2 Cor 5¹⁷).

Thus he comes to the joy of forgiveness. Repentance is often
spoken of as a gloomy thing, but what could be more full of
utter gladness than to see oneself as one really is, and then to
discover that all is forgiven and the intimacy with God is
restored (cf. Lk 15). Out of the crushing desolation of a
recognition of sin, springs at the mere whisper of the Father's
pardoning love the rapture of the soul restored to its God
(verses 8, 12).

In this joyful certainty the psalmist makes his vows. He will
tell others of the salvation he has found—rich experience leads
to ardent evangelism (verse 13). He will sing aloud God's
praises—the Church of pardoned sinners exult in their Saviour
(verses 14–15, cf. **40³**). He will offer himself, humble, contrite,

his self-will crushed, as the only sacrifice God desires (verses
16–17; cf. 34[18], Isa 57[15], 66[2]).

The last two verses seem to be the addition of a later Jew
who wanted to correct the impression that God did not require
the sacrifice ordained in the law. When Jerusalem is rebuilt
after the exile, then God will take pleasure in the offerings of
His people.

52. A Prophetic Denunciation

Abruptly the writer of this psalm enters upon a fierce invective
against a powerful opponent whose slanders are an affront
to God (verses 1–4). After uttering a threat of his destruction
and contrasting the blessing which comes to those who trust
in God (verses 5–8), he ends with a thanksgiving (verse 9).

52[1]. The poetry of this verse has faulty rhythm and paral-
lelism. It is better to alter slightly as *RSV*.

> 'Why do you boast, O mighty man,
>   of mischief done against the godly?
>   All the day you are plotting destruction.'

52[4]. '*devouring words*'. Rather, 'words of slander'.

52[5]. '*take thee up*'. The verb probably means, 'knock down,
destroy'.

52[7]. '*wickedness*'. Perhaps read 'wealth' with the Aramaic
and Syriac versions (as *RSV*).

52[9]. '*I will wait on*'. A small emendation gives, 'I will proclaim' (as *RSV*), but the word may have the extended meaning
of, 'I will show respect to'.

This is best understood in the light of Isaiah's denunciation
of Shebna (Isa 22[15–19], cf. Jer 20[3–6], 28[15–16], Amos 7[16–17]).
It is not mere personal antagonism and more is involved than
conflicting policies. The prophet is so certain that he knows
the mind of God that those who oppose him are held to be
working against Him. God will destroy them as evil-doers.
Even if this psalm has its origin in party strife, the doings

of the '*mighty man*' are plainly wicked, for he is using the power which his wealth gives to spread slanderous lies to the injury of others. Verse 5 is thus not a curse or a prayer, but expresses the prophetic word foretelling God's judgement.

Over against the fate of the wicked, the blessing of the psalmist is to know prosperity in the presence of God. He likens himself to a luxuriant olive tree growing in the temple court, much as cypresses and olives grow in the area of the Dome of the Rock today.

This psalm does not seem to have been used in the services of the Synagogue, and it is questionable whether it is fitting to sing it in Christian worship. Yet, despite its violence, it bears witness to important truths.

(*a*) There is judgement upon evil. As often in the OT, this is worked out in this present world. Although the nature of the judgement needs to be redefined, it is not superseded by the revelation of Christ (cf. Mt 13[24-30], [36-43], [47-50], 25[31-46]). A sign of the acknowledgement of God's sovereignty is the acquiescence in and acceptance of His judgement.

(*b*) To a world where the degrees of the seriousness of sins are often grievously confused, this psalm bears witness to the evil of the sins of dishonesty and slander. God does not overlook the innuendo which destroys a reputation, the deliberate lie or cruel truth which causes bitter division, the deceptions of political propaganda, commercial advertisement and the packaging of goods, the debauchery of sensational journalism. Where language is abused and truth corrupted, faith and trust are extinguished and fellowship between men rendered impossible.

53. God's Help for the Righteous in a Corrupt World

See on 14.

54. 'Save me, O God, by thy name'

The psalmist, threatened by ruthless and godless enemies, prays to Yahweh for help, confident that He will support and deliver him. This may be the plea of one accused of some wrong (see on 7, and note '*judge*'—'vindicate'—in verse 1), although there is no declaration of innocence. It is, indeed, rather idle to speculate on the exact nature of the distress from which the psalmist seeks deliverance.

54¹. *'by thy name'*; i.e. the character of Yahweh, active in His world and powerful to save. His nature and His name is love.

54⁴. *'of them that uphold'*. Rather, 'the great Upholder'. *RV* (and *RSV* with its needless emendation) has misunderstood the syntax and obscured a theological truth. God is not one among many helpers the psalmist may have; He is the great Supporter of his life. So also in **118⁷**, 'Yahweh is my great Helper'.

Apart from the apparently vindictive spirit shown by the writer—a vindictiveness readily understood when it is remembered that the eternal issues of God's justice had to be worked out upon the very restricted stage of one human lifetime, and that the psalmist regarded his enemies as evil men and therefore the enemies also of Yahweh (cf. **5** and see further on **69**)—this is a model petition for help. A cry to God is followed by a brief description of the danger which threatens (verses 1–2, 3). Having laid his cause before Yahweh the psalmist leaves it there, no longer troubled in his heart, and sings only of the great Supporter in whom he places his confidence. So sure is he that his prayer is heard, that he turns immediately to speak of the freewill offering, the one sacrifice which expressed the voluntary gratitude of a thankful heart, which he will bring to God (verses 4–7). This is prayer which asks, believing that it has received (Mk 11²⁴).

55. 'I am distraught by the noise of the enemy'

Sudden changes of thought and an alternation between a single enemy and groups of oppressors, together with an alleged difference of background in various parts of the psalm, have led to suggestions of composite authorship; but there is little agreement as to how it should be divided up and it is best treated as a unity. Moreover, although the psalm is the lament of an individual, there is uncertainty about its exact nature. If the enemies were those hurling false accusations against the psalmist, it might be a plea for divine vindication (cf. **7**). More probably it comes from a time of civil unrest, when law and order have broken down and there is a general collapse of moral standards (note verses 9–11).

55⁸⁻⁹ᵃ. With a small rearrangement to suit the rhythm and some vowel changes these lines may be rendered,

> 'I will haste me to a refuge
>   from a spirit of calumny,
>   from the storm of slander, O Lord,
>   and the strife of their tongues.'

55¹⁹. '*who have no changes*'. The exact significance is uncertain. Perhaps, 'vicissitudes of fortune' (they do not fear God because they have had unbroken prosperity), or, 'mutual obligations' (they reveal their depravity by breaking faith).

After an appeal to be heard (verses 1–2), the psalmist tells of the anguish of mind and dire straits into which he has been brought by the attacks of his enemies (verses 3–5). He had contemplated flight (verses 6–9a), for the city is seething with civil strife and deeds of violence, with acts of oppression and fraud (verses 9b–11). Even his friend has turned against him (verses 12–14). He breaks off with a curse (verse 15). But he realizes that to run away is no escape; the true way out is to turn to God (verses 16–19). Yet even as he prays, his thought wanders back to the treachery of his friend (verses 20–1). Perhaps he recalls, in verse 22, the word of a temple priest giving the assurance that Yahweh will never let a good man come to grief. The psalm ends in confident trust.

To many it may appear that three verses of great beauty and rich with associations (verses 6, 16, 22) are sunk in the middle of a poem devoted to an almost pagan desire for revenge. Yet once the apparent vindictiveness is understood (see on **5, 54, 69**), the psalm is seen to express an important truth.

How does a man react when the foundations of ordered social life are crumbling, and friendships are found to be too weak to stand the strains to which they are now subjected? Centuries of the strong rule of law have made us less ready to appreciate the need for a stable and just government. Thomas Hobbes was born in troubled times and said of himself, 'Fear and I were twins'. He trembled at the thought of anarchy and pictured it vividly. When men seek only their own selfish ends there can be no security. Agriculture, industry and commerce are brought to a standstill. There can be 'No Arts; no Letters; no Society; and, which is worst of all,

H

continuall feare, and danger of violent death'. This is the situation in which the psalmist finds himself. Violence and strife stalk through the city, the weak are ruthlessly oppressed, honesty has disappeared. No friend can be trusted, not even where the friendship had been cemented by ties of affection, religion, and the most solemn bonds, and where there has been a mutual opening up of the inmost thoughts of the heart (cf. 41⁹).

Where does such a man turn? If he is in a position of authority, he tries to reassert the standards that lie in ruins around him. But if he is one without any influence or power? The temptation is to get away, out of it all. 'O, for the wings of a dove!' Mendelssohn's music must not lull our spirits that they overlook the irreligious escapism of the desire. The psalmist, despite his fears and anguish of heart, stays where he is and throws himself upon God's protection. '*As for me, I will call upon God.*' Here is the setting of the jewel verse, '*Cast thy burden on the Lord, and he shall sustain thee*'. The word for '*burden*' only occurs here, and seems to mean, 'what is given, thy lot', the cares and anxieties which lie so heavily upon the psalmist. Cast it all upon Yahweh and He will '*sustain*'—not deliver, not provide a way out, but give the strength to endure. Three Greek translations give a reading which is hardly original, although it is adopted by Moffatt, but which none-the-less expresses the ground of this confidence, 'Leave all to the Eternal, *who loves you*'. (The whole psalm should be compared with **11.**)

There have been times in the history of the Church when violence and wrong seemed to rule the world and it looked as if the Christian virtues would be crushed out of existence. At these times, some Christians fled to the monasteries and the desert. Probably they preserved learning and civilization and kept alive the ideal of the holy life. Others stayed where they were, often compromising, sometimes becoming as corrupt as their neighbours, occasionally suffering martyrdom, but show-ing that the Christian life must be lived in the world. Because of their presence, much cruelty was softened and much vice restrained. It is not without significance that the writer of 1 Peter quotes verse 22 of this psalm as an encouragement to Christians upon whom the fiery trial was just coming (1 Pet 5⁷).

56. 'When I am afraid, I put my trust in thee'

Little more can be ascertained about this psalm than that it is
another individual lament, seeking help against persecuting
enemies. There seems little reason to class it with the prayers
of those falsely accused, and the petition against the *'peoples'*
in verse 7 is insufficient to make it certain that it was offered
by a king threatened by foreign enemies, or by one of the Jews
of the dispersion who had to face early outbreaks of anti-
Semitism.

Similarities with other individual laments can be seen in the
deep trust in God, the prayers for the destruction of the
enemies, their malice recoiling upon their own heads, and
the change to thanksgiving at the end, revealing the confidence that the prayer is heard.

The text and exact translation is frequently uncertain and
RV may be compared with *RSV*.

56[8]. *'my wanderings'*. Perhaps, 'my sleeplessness'.

Early interpretations of this psalm are of interest. The title
was clearly added by an editor who regarded it as the prayer
of an individual, for he tried to provide a suitable occasion
for its composition in the life of David. The Greek translation, however, paraphrased part of that title as, 'For the people
removed far from the sanctuary'. The Aramaic version has,
'Concerning the congregation of Israel, which is compared to a
silent dove at the time when they were far from their cities,
and turned again and praised the Lord of the World'. Both
show that it was treated as a national psalm spoken by a personified people. In recent times, many of the psalms were
interpreted in this way, but if the cultic setting is correct they
must be regarded as being offered by a single Israelite, although
not as being the personal experience of an individual poet.

The Christian will treasure the psalmist's confidence in God.
Men are mere feeble flesh compared with Him (cf. Isa 31[1-3]).
Picturesquely he imagines Yahweh storing up his tears. With
such a God there is no place for fear (verses 3 and 11; see
Mt 6[25-34], 10[28-31], Lk 12[32]).

And while the psalmist can only expect deliverance from
sudden or premature death, Yahweh still preserving his life in
the regions of light and prosperity, those who have seen that

Jesus is the Light of the world discover that to follow Him is to enjoy the true 'light of life' (verse 13, *RV*m, and Jn 8[12]).

57. Prayer and Thanksgiving

This psalm falls into two sections, a prayer for deliverance from slanderous enemies (verses 1–6), and thanksgiving which almost turns into a hymn of praise (verses 7–11). The supposition that these are two distinct psalms, or perhaps fragments of psalms, gains some support from the recurrence of the second part as 108[1-5]. On the other hand there is a refrain in verses 5 and 11, and while there is no mention of enemies in verses 7–11 there are similarities of style with the earlier verses. It may, therefore, be treated as a unity.

57[3-4]. It has been suggested that these lines should be read,

'May He send from heaven to save me,
    having disappointed them that pant after my life.
In the midst of lions must I lie down,
    who devour the sons of men.'

57[6]. '*My soul is bowed down*'. Perhaps the meaning is, 'My soul turned aside',—I avoided it.

57[8]. '*my glory*'. Cf. 16[9] and 108[1]. Some think the original was, 'Thou art my glory'.

This psalm presents the same difficulties of interpretation as **56**, to which it is somewhat akin. It appears to be a prayer offered before sunrise. Several features apparently connected with the Jerusalem temple, such as '*the shadow of thy wings*', '*God most High*', Yahweh's '*glory*', and the reference to the nations, make more plausible the suggestion that it was composed for those accused of some crime who were spending the night in the temple—though this is far from certain. On this reconstruction, the psalmist lies down in the sanctuary to await the divine judgement, having uttered his urgent, yet trustful, prayer. When he has received this vindication he rises to sing his praises, accompanied by stringed instruments, to the One who saves at dawn (cf. **17**).

Whatever the exact nature of the danger which threatened

the psalmist, his confident faith and eager praise shine out.
He trusts himself to the gracious love of Yahweh, the Most
High, who is God, exalted above the heavens, His glory
spreading over all the earth. The mercy of God does not
diminish His majestic power; indeed, it depends upon it. And
when a man has received God's vindication, his immediate
response is joyous thanksgiving (cf. the thanksgivings in
Paul's letters, or the doxologies in *Revelation*).

58. 'Verily there is a God that judgeth in the earth'

This psalm does not fit readily into any of the main classes.
The denunciation of the wicked is similar to the prophetic
invective of **52,** while the background conception of the unjust
rule of subordinate deities (if this is the meaning of verse 1, see
below) links it with **82.** The dominant theme is that Yahweh's
justice will prevail over evil.

58¹. '*in silence*'. If this is the correct translation of a very
obscure word, the sense apparently is that the judges are
failing in their duty to pronounce just sentences. A change in
the vowels would give either 'nobles', the wicked in high places
who are perverting justice by their tyrannous rule, or 'gods',
who are responsible under Yahweh for maintaining justice in
the world (see **82**). The Greek version and Jerome, however,
seem to have read the word with still other vowels as 'then' or
'certainly'.

58². *RSV* follows several of the ancient versions with its,

> 'Nay, in your hearts you devise wrongs;
> your hands deal out violence on earth.'

It has been suggested that the meaning is,

> 'Nay, but right heartily do ye wreak deeds of injustice in the
> world,
> and scrutinize the violence of your hands'—to see its effect
> in the world.

58⁷ᵇ. *RV* is questionable and the Hebrew almost unin-
telligible. A plausible alteration gives, 'like grass which is
crushed down let them wither away' (cf. *RSV*).

58⁸⁻⁹. No satisfactory sense can be obtained from the present text. If *RV* of verse 8a is retained, the idea is either that snails were thought to melt away in the slimy trail they leave, or it is a reference to their drying up in time of drought. But perhaps the two verses should be rendered,

> 'Like a miscarriage which melteth away,
>> like the untimely fruit of a woman they shall not see the sun.
> Ere they perceive it, he will pull them up like thorns,
>> like weeds, in his wrath he will sweep them away.'

The startling and vivid imagery of this psalm, combined with the ferocity of verse 10, present serious difficulties to the modern reader. There is no doubt that it belongs to a different era and has not been baptized into the spirit of Christ. Yet it would be a pity if its strangeness should be a barrier to the truth it proclaims, and while it is unsuitable for normal Christian worship, it deserves the serious attention of the preacher.

The writer is living at a time when justice is flagrantly violated under a corrupt tyranny. Wicked men are able to pursue their evil designs unhindered. It seems almost as though the beings who have charge of the world have become perverted, and instead of securing justice have turned to work evil with malignant zest. A good man is powerless; his most strenuous efforts, even enchantments, are useless against this determined wickedness.

But appeal may still be made to Yahweh. Verses 6–9 have been described as a sevenfold curse upon the wicked. This is a misrepresentation. When everything seems awry and goodness has lost all power, man can only seek the judgement of God. The verses are an urgent appeal to Him, unless they are an expression of prophetic certainty that He will quell this onrush of wickedness.

Thus faith wins through. The psalm ends with confidence that morality is secure. The subjugation of evil gives exultant joy to the righteous as they see goodness vindicated and God supreme.

There have been golden periods in history when society seemed stable and unchanging, when the coarser passions and cruel lusts of men were held in check, and the prevalent

humanity and virtue were thought to be the natural growth of a
developing enlightenment. At other times the barriers are
down, and civilization is seen to be a thin and brittle veneer
which is quite unable to restrain injustices and wickedness
which stagger the mind and send a man back reeling. It is in
such times that those who are slaughtered for the testimony
they bear cry out, 'O Sovereign Lord, holy and true, how long
before thou wilt judge and avenge our blood?' And when the
judgement is given, the cry goes up, 'Hallelujah! Salvation and
glory and power belong to our God, for his judgements are
true and just' (Rev 6[10], 19[1-2], *RSV*). There *is* a God. The
universe is not oblivious to right and wrong, and men are not
in the grip of omnipotent wickedness. Love is stronger than
hatred, goodness will defeat evil and righteousness be triumphant. (On the necessity of accepting God's judgement of
sin, see **18** and **52**.)

59. Yahweh the Fortress of the Persecuted

This is the prayer of one persecuted and slanderously wronged.

59[7]. '*swords*'. It is suggested that the word really means
'deceit', although *RV* can be understood from **57[4]**.

59[11]. The meaning is that Yahweh should not destroy the
wicked too quickly, lest their evil deeds be forgotten and the
justice of God's rule not fully appreciated (cf. Ezek 12[16]). But
there is some doubt about the text of verses 11–13.

59[14-15]. This is hardly a refrain (see verses 6–7). Some think
it is a variant of the previous occurrence. If it is original here,
it should probably be regarded as a description of the enemies
rather than a curse upon them.

The exact nature of this individual lament is difficult to
determine. The attacks of adversaries and assertions of innocence suggest that it may be the prayer of an accused man who
seeks help in the temple, and perhaps awaits God's word of
vindication after a night vigil (see verses 1–4, 16). The mention
of foreign nations in verses 5 and 8, however, gives some ground
for the suggestion that this is a national petition or the prayer
of the king as leader of his people, though the words may
come from the usages of the Jerusalem cultus.

It is hardly suitable for use in Christian worship, since many phrases are open to serious misunderstanding. The psalmist's attitude towards his enemies is not merely a thirst for vengeance. It arises from his certainty that their accusations are false and unjust and from his belief that those who oppose him are also Yahweh's enemies (see further on **69**). However, the very vigour of the language obscures this. A striking feature of the psalm is its confidence in God, who is described as the '*high tower*', the fortress and defence of the one in need.

60. A Divine Word in a time of National Disaster

In defeat the people raise this lament and a prophet utters a message from Yahweh. (Verses 5–12 recur as **108⁶⁻¹³**.)

60³. Perhaps,

> 'Thou hast made Thy people drunk with sour wine,
> Thou hast made us to imbibe intoxicating drink.'

60⁴ᵇ. The meaning is probably as *RV*m, in a tone of sarcasm.

60⁵ᵇ. 'Open wide Thy right hand and answer us.'

60⁶. '*in his holiness*', or 'in His sanctuary'.

60⁸ᶜ. Probably the original was as **108⁹**; 'over Philistia I shout in triumph' (as *RSV*).

The armies of Israel have been defeated and the people flee in panic. God seems to have turned against them in fierce anger. The disaster is pictured as a devastating earthquake or the reelings of drunken men. With bitter sarcasm the people exclaim that Yahweh led them out to war only to compass their ruin.

Verses 6–8, which are marked off from the rest of the psalm by the metre, contain the words of a prophet, probably a temple official who had the duty to deliver a divine message in times such as this. He proclaims the sovereignty of Yahweh over His own land, and over the surrounding states which had been subject to Israel in the reign of David.

Yet the people return to their lament. They seek divine

protection as they go into Edom, either as fugitives or as an attacking army. Only in the last verse is there any confidence or certainty of success.

There seems little that is even distinctively Israelite in this psalm, for Mesha, king of Moab, writes of his defeat in the same terms, saying that 'Omri, king of Israel, afflicted Moab for many days because Chemosh was angry with his land', but later saved him and let him see his pleasure on all them that hated him. And the naked idea of Yahweh as God of battling armies is alien to Christian thought. The prophetic oracle might almost be quoted as an example of what cannot be read in services of public worship today. A comparison even with a psalm like **44** shows the spiritual poverty here. The most that can be said is that it belongs to a less enlightened stage of Israel's life, but that even at this stage the need of complete reliance upon God was being learnt and His universal sovereignty over the whole of the world's life being perceived.

61. Prayer in Confident Assurance

This individual lament is marked by trust in God. Verses 6–7 contain a prayer for the king.

61^{2b}. The meaning may be, 'the rock that is too high for me' —I cannot reach it in my own strength. Some would follow the Greek version; 'Lift me up upon a rock and make me secure.'

61^{5}. *'heritage'*. A very small alteration would give 'request'.

The note of confidence in God's loving protection, and the closing vow to live a life of daily thanksgiving, make this psalm so attractive that it is of lesser moment that ambiguities of interpretation remain. Briefly, there are two difficulties. (1) It is uncertain what is the distress which has befallen the psalmist. Is he an exile? Or does verse 2 simply express his sense of separation from God which his suffering brings? Or is he near to death? (2) The prayer for the king comes very abruptly. Is the whole psalm offered by the king, with verses 6–7 perhaps spoken by a choir? Or does the Israelite psalmist, like the Babylonian, break off abruptly into a prayer for the king? Or are these verses a later interpolation? No certain

solution of these problems can be found—and it matters
little, for here is one who has moved far into the secrets of
prayer.

Distress has come to the psalmist, yet he does not give way
to whinings and moanings. Indeed, so lightly does he touch
upon his sufferings that they remain obscure. He puts away
all thoughts of himself as he turns to God. Even though
Yahweh seems far off, he prays with an almost joyful certainty. He is his refuge and defence. In His temple there is
security. On the character of Yahweh he relies. His unwavering faithfulness and enduring love are a secure stronghold.
Thus gratitude crowns the psalm. Not vows paid in a moment
and as swiftly forgotten will be his response to Yahweh's
goodness. His thankfulness issues in continual praise.

62. Quiet Confidence

Attacked by enemies and in great distress, the psalmist expresses his utter trust in God. He is a sure refuge at all times.

62³. *'That ye may slay him'*. Some alter to 'will you rush at
him', a small change.

62⁴. Minor alterations would give,

> 'They plan only deceptions,
> They delight in leading astray.
> Falsely they bless with their mouth
> But in their heart they curse.'

62¹¹. *'once, twice'*. The numbers are not intended to be
exact. This is a common way of laying emphasis and is found
not only in other Israelite writings (cf. Job 33¹⁴, 40⁵), but also
in the literatures of other ancient Near Eastern peoples.

Vigorously the psalmist depicts the onslaught of his enemies.
With slanders and curses they aim at securing his downfall.
A deliberate hypocrisy is theirs, which outwardly shows friendship and claims to desire the psalmist's good, but inwardly
only seeks his destruction (verse 3–4).

Yet, where others meet evil with burning invective and match
their opponents' curses with their own, this psalmist shows a

calm assurance of God's protection hardly rivalled in the whole Psalter. His response to the hostile attacks is to turn in quiet confidence to God. He is Rock and Salvation, Fortress and Refuge, and on Him the afflicted may set his hope. Crushed beyond the help of words, he waits, in silent longing for God's help. 'My soul is silence, waiting all hushed for God' (E. A. Leslie).

But when a man finds God, he must help others in a distress like his own. '*Trust in him at all times, ye people*' (the Greek has 'all the congregation of the people'). God's care is not reserved for any special group, nor are there periods when men must stand alone. In Him is the true security, not in human power or earthly resources, for His power consists of all the massive resources of love—the Christian has seen how costly the expenditure of these resources can be (verses 8–12).

Even before Christ had come to show the perfect way of meeting the malice and hostility of evil men, there were those who did not render evil for evil or reviling for reviling. If they failed to attain the summit of asking blessing on their persecutors, they showed the way of accepting suffering patiently and keeping a firm faith in God's loving care (see 1 Pet 2²⁰⁻⁴, 3⁸⁻⁹).

63. 'Thy steadfast love is better than life'

Deep longing for God and trust in His love are strikingly apparent in this prayer of one persecuted and afflicted.

63¹. '*early will I seek thee*'. So the Greek version translated this verb, connecting it with the word for morning. Hence this psalm was widely used in the Christian Church as a morning hymn. Chrysostom says, 'The Fathers of the Church appointed it to be said every morning, as a spiritual song and a medicine to blot out our sins; to kindle in us a desire of God; to raise our souls, and inflame them with a mighty fire of devotion; to make us overflow with goodness and love, and send us with such preparation to approach and appear before God.' Although the verb probably means 'seek' simply, the words of Chrysostom well express the value of the psalm for the devotional life.

The exact setting of this lament is uncertain. Some suppose that the first verse indicates that the psalmist is an exile, but

the words are probably metaphorical and reveal his feeling of
desolation. Verse 11 suggests that it is the king who is praying,
but the worshipper might include the king in his prayers. All
that is certain is that this psalm is intended for those who seek
refuge in God and His deliverance before their enemies.
Perhaps such a one has fled to the sanctuary.

No one can miss the eagerness with which this psalmist
looks for God. With all his being he thirsts for Him and faints
with longing. In the past he has experienced Yahweh's power
and glory in the temple (verse 2). It was not only the great
prophet to whom the temple became resplendent with God's
glory. This psalm shows that the ordinary Israelite could have
the same sense of the divine majesty.

Verse 3 is the most precious gem in a psalm that is rich with
treasures. Its setting in ancient Israel enhances its splendour.
In an age when death meant the end of all that was of value
and the passing into the gloom of Sheol, and among a people
who saw God's richest blessing in a long and prosperous life,
this psalmist asserts that better even than life itself is Yahweh's
unwavering love. Here is security. Here is the sure foundation.

Hence he turns to glad thanksgiving and joyous praise. As
throughout the NT, the thought of God's grace brings a man
inevitably to a thanksgiving which not only drives out sadness
but also quells all fears. The enemies and their threatenings
are forgotten in the wonder of God's goodness. A feeling of
security that is free from all anxiety is given by the conviction
of God's nearness. 'It is not given to all to have such faith;
but even to hear of it is an inspiration, and an incentive to
draw nearer to God' (Oesterley).

Many will feel that verses 9–11 are a lamentable anticlimax
at the end of an intensely spiritual psalm. They show, however, that this is not the prayer of a solitary contemplative,
aloof from the strains of daily living, but is intended for those
who must daily battle amid the pressures of the world and face
the hostility of implacable foes. For most of us faith and
prayer and any experience of God which we hope to have must
be found within the everyday, not by withdrawal from it. Yet,
as the psalmist comes seeking deliverance from his enemies, he
can only imagine security with their death. It is a strange and
frightening fact that the most beautiful devotion can exist
alongside sentiments and passions that seem far distant from

the character of the God who is being worshipped. Society moulds our moral attitudes far more than we realize, and the writer of this psalm shows himself as the child of his age.

64. A Prayer for Help

Though menaced by vicious enemies, the psalmist is certain that Yahweh will deliver him. Unfortunately the text is corrupt in several verses.

As in other laments, one who is convinced of his innocence (see verse 4) pleads for help as he is threatened by opponents bent on his destruction. He says that their words are sharp arrows, and probably it is their curses which he fears. The Israelite believed that the spoken word had effective power in itself. Thus Isaac was unable to recall or alter the blessing which he had mistakenly pronounced upon Jacob (Gen 27), while the curses found in the law books are no empty words, but are intended to bring the misfortunes which they announce upon those who break the commandments. Against this the psalmist is powerless. Only Yahweh can annul the evil designs of the enemies and save him. And because he watches over the innocent and knows the secret plots of the wicked, He will deliver him. *They* had spoken the word which would bring his destruction. *Yahweh* will speak the word which will crush them. This will be a sure proof of His effective justice, and while all men stand in awe the righteous will be enheartened and rejoice.

There is little here that evokes any response from the modern Christian. The ideas set the psalm in a distant age. Its spirit separates it by a wide gulf from the Christian way. Yet we should not too easily pass by a faith which is certain that there is no situation so desperate, no opposition so powerful and determined, no weakness so complete, that God cannot intervene. The Christian, however, knows that God's intervention is not with a word of retaliation, but with the Word of reconciliation, and that the wounds are not inflicted upon the enemies, but are accepted by the Son.

65. The Goodness of God

The congregation at the Jerusalem temple praises Yahweh as the One who forgives sin, as the great Creator, and as the Giver of fruitfulness to the earth.

65¹. '*waiteth for thee*'. The word '*waiteth*' seems rather to be the noun 'silence', and although there may be moments of rapt adoration when

> *A sacred reverence checks our songs*
> *And praise sits silent on our tongues,*

this hardly seems a suitable thought at the beginning of a hymn. Probably the tradition which adopted different vowels should be followed; 'Praise is due to thee' (as *RSV*).

65²ᵇ⁻³. *RV* follows the verse division of the original, but the poetic rhythm favours the *RSV*:

> 'To thee shall all flesh come
>   on account of sins.
> When our transgressions prevail over us,
>   thou dost forgive them.'

Men's sins are too heavy a matter for them to deal with, but God is ready to forgive.

65⁴. This is said of the priests in Numbers 16⁵—but all God's people are priests and can approach Him.

65⁵. '*in righteousness*'. *RSV*, 'with deliverance', expresses the sense.

It is not certain when this hymn was sung in ancient Israel. The references to the primeval deep and to Yahweh as Creator might seem to link it with the great autumn festival. However, the harvest does not appear to have been gathered in, and it is easier to regard it as a spring song, when the winter rains have saturated the fields and given the promise of abundant crops. It falls into three distinct sections (verses 1–4, 5–8, and 9–13), but there is no need to suppose that it is made up of separate poems.

The opening verses praise Yahweh for His goodness in forgiving the sin of His people. In the temple they can meet and worship Him, knowing that He hears their prayers and accepts their vows, and removes their sin so that it no longer prevents full and open fellowship with Him. To those who have discovered this, worship is no routine duty. The congregation sings of the happiness of the man whom God welcomes into His presence. They approach God with a deep sense of privilege, confident that He will give full satisfaction of all their needs.

Men come to God because they owe Him vows, and because they want Him to answer their prayers, and because they are conscious of their sin, and because they know He forgives sin, and because He invites them and draws them to Himself, and because there is blessing in His presence. They praise Him simply because He is *God*.

Beside the tender forgiveness of God, there is His awe-inspiring majesty. The psalm fills out the picture of the great Creator with old-world ideas (cf. **24**$^{1-2}$). Yahweh can quell the destructive tumult of the ancient deep. His mighty power is seen in the mountains which He has firmly established. Thus those who live at the farthest bounds of the earth are filled with awe at His deeds, and the uttermost parts of east and west shout their joyful praise. And this God saves those who pray to Him. The dread deeds of deliverance perhaps contain a reminiscence of the Exodus, though the reference is chiefly to a present salvation.

Only after the goodness of God and His majestic power have been described do the worshippers mention the immediate cause of their rejoicing. God has given abundant rain, that rain which alone can make the dry ground fertile, give life to the seed and save the nation from famine. Again old-world pictures are used. The mighty river, which was thought to surround the earth and flow outside the dome of heaven, is under Yahweh's control, and provides the rains. Yahweh's wagon drives across the land, leaving behind it a trail of fruitfulness. Everywhere there is rich abundance.

This attractive psalm expresses praise that springs from a rich understanding of God and His ways with men. The sequence of thought is significant. Forgiveness is not tacked on as an afterthought. The psalmist realizes that intimacy with God is the highest blessing, and that this can only be found at God's invitation and after He has cleansed men from their sin. When a man possesses this familiarity with God, he can bow down before His glory as it is revealed in nature and give thanks for His goodness shown in the good fruits of the earth.

66. Praise, National Thanksgiving, and Personal Gratitude

This psalm falls into three sections. Verses 1–7 are a hymn of
praise to Yahweh, in which the Exodus and the crossing of the
Jordan are specially mentioned; verses 8–12 contain a national
thanksgiving for a more recent deliverance; and the final
section of the psalm is an individual thanksgiving for an
answer to prayer. It seems somewhat forced to regard the
speaker in this last part as the nation Israel, and it is not,
therefore, surprising that suggestions of composite authorship
have been made.

66⁶. *'there'*. Does this mean that the psalm was sung at the
site of the crossing of the Jordan? Perhaps it comes from the
sanctuary at Gilgal. Or later Israel may be identifying itself
with the nation which God saved at the Exodus.

66¹⁰, ¹². Cf. Isaiah 43², 48¹⁰, 51²³. Some think that similarities such as these show that the psalm is post-exilic and refers
to the return from exile in Babylon.

66¹⁷ᵇ. A small change would give, 'And I was raised from
under my foes' (*AT*).

66¹⁸. God will accept any prayer, if only it be sincere.

The hymn with which the psalm opens calls on the whole earth
to shout the praises of Yahweh. His power is so great that
even those who hate Him must yield an unwilling and outward
obedience as they cringe before Him. The faith of Israel was
centred in the Exodus and the conquest of Palestine, for it was
in this deliverance that the wonder of His love for His people
was most clearly seen (see Deut 26⁵⁻⁹), and it is this which the
congregation now recalls.

The section of thanksgiving speaks of the dangers through
which the nation has passed. These were a time when their
faith and loyalty to Yahweh were tested. It might be that
the broad sweep of Israel's history is held in view, though
some more specific deliverance seems to be intended. The
terms in which it is described, however, are too general for us

to be able to fit it to any particular occasion. Perhaps this is because it was meant to be used on any occasion of national thanksgiving.

At verse 13, an individual says that he has come to fulfil the vows which he had made when he was in trouble. To these vows he now adds other sacrifices, so great is his thankfulness. His gratitude expresses itself in witness as well as in offerings. The faith of those who serve God will be strengthened as they hear of some new expression of His goodness. He has answered prayer and surrounded one of His worshippers with His grace.

The relation of these sections to each other is uncertain.

(1) They may have been originally quite separate, being combined by a later editor. Thus perhaps verses 1–7 were sung at a festival at Gilgal when the Exodus and entry into Canaan were celebrated. The middle section may be a continuation of this, or be a psalm to be sung at a time of national rejoicing. The individual thanksgiving would then have been written as the prayer for those who come to the temple to repay their vows.

(2) The whole psalm may be a national thanksgiving. The final section would be spoken by the king or some other leader of the people.

(3) An individual might have prefixed to his own thanksgiving a hymn that strictly applied to the nation.

(4) It may even be that this psalm is a liturgy, and that it was during a temple service of thanksgiving that an individual came forward to express his own gratitude.

Whatever its earlier history may have been, however, this psalm has been handed down to us in its present form, and the message which it expresses as a whole should not be overlooked. Praise and gratitude are keynotes of Jewish and Christian worship, and since it is by His past salvation that God has revealed His character to men, we must cry, 'Come and see what God has done' (verse 5, *RSV*). But His salvation does not belong only to the distant past, and we need not simply look back rather wistfully as we offer our praise. He is a God who is still active in His world and still saves. Faith is grounded on what God has done, whether in the Exodus or in the Incarnation; faith lives by seeing what God is doing today. And in this faith we offer our individual thanksgiving. Personal religion is more than private prayer or secret vow, and God is known, not only through personal experience, but also through the historical revelation.

67. A Prayer at Harvest-time

'*The earth hath yielded her increase*'. This is clearly to be sung at the time of harvest, though it opens with a prayer for God's blessing.

67¹. '*God be merciful*'; rather, 'May God be gracious' (as *RSV*).

67⁶. '*God, even our own God*'. In **42–83** an editor seems to have changed an original 'Yahweh' to '*God*'. Hence here the congregation probably sang, 'Yahweh, our God, will bless us,' or even, 'May Yahweh, our God, bless us'.

A refrain in verses 3 and 5 divides the psalm into three parts.

The opening recalls the priestly blessing in Numbers 6²⁴⁻⁶. The grace of God and the joys of fellowship with Him are sought, yet not as delights to be selfishly hoarded, but in order that the non-Jewish nations may see Yahweh's salvation and live that good life which He both requires and offers. Thus God's gracious dealings with Israel will lead all men to give to Him their worship.

Verse 4 expresses the thought of Yahweh's just rule over the whole world. '*judge*' is not 'condemn', but 'govern' and 'vindicate'. The word translated '*govern*' is really 'lead', a word often used of Yahweh's loving guidance of His people (see Ex 13¹⁷, ²¹, 15¹³, Isa 57¹⁸, 58¹¹), and only here applied to His caring for foreign nations (contrast Job 12²³).

Only at verse 6 do we discover that the people have come to offer their thanksgiving for the harvest, and even then the psalm quickly turns to confident assurance of God's continuing blessing, or reverts to the earlier prayer. As the Israelite came to the temple with gratitude in his heart for the good gifts of the earth, he realized that God is infinitely more precious than His gifts (cf. Deut 26¹⁻¹¹, where the harvest festival is the occasion for reciting the Israelite creed which is centred on the Exodus deliverance). So in the NT there is joyful thanksgiving on every hand, and no loss of faith in God as the Creator; yet when Paul thanks God for His 'gift beyond words' (2 Cor 9¹⁵, *NEB*) it is, as always, Christ to whom he refers.

Throughout this psalm the narrow confines of the nation are burst asunder. It is Yahweh, the God of Israel, who has given the harvest to His people, but the congregation looks for His righteous dominion over the whole world and to praises being offered by all men. The blessing Israel has received makes them a missionary people, and contains the hope that those who see His goodness will come to worship Him. This is the true motive for evangelism—not the fear that men may die without Christ, but the grief that they continue to live without the happiness of knowing Him.

68. The Triumph of Yahweh

This is the most difficult of all the psalms; yet it is a fine hymn which repays the effort required to understand it. There are broadly two lines of interpretation. Some, impressed by the frequent changes of subject and the many allusions to other poems in the OT, have thought that it is a collection of short, independent songs, or even an index or catalogue of poems. Others find in it an essential unity, the apparent breaks in the thought being due to the movement of the ritual with which it was sung, or to the interweaving of diverse themes in the worship. The attractive reconstruction of Aubrey Johnson, who accepts the unity of the psalm, is here closely followed. Difficulties in the text do not make it any easier to understand, and some alternative translations, mostly from Aubrey Johnson, are listed below.

68¹. Rather, 'When God ariseth, His enemies are scattered . . .'. This is a statement of fact, not petition. The reference seems to be to the carrying of the ark in procession (cf. **24** and Num 10³⁵).

68⁶. 'God giveth the lonely a home wherein to dwell' (cf. *RV*m and *RSV*).

68⁸. 'The earth quaked, the heavens poured down rain,
   Before Yahweh, Him of Sinai, before Yahweh, the God
      of Israel.'

68[13a]. 'If you lie down between the saddle-bags'—like a stubborn or lazy donkey. The rest of the verse probably describes a choice item of spoil.

68[15]. 'O mighty mountain, mountain of Bashan;
    O many-peaked (or lofty) mountain, mountain of Bashan' (cf. *RSV*).

68[17b]. 'The Lord is among them, the God of Sinai is in the sanctuary.'

68[18c]. 'Even those who rebelled at Yahweh's choice of a home.'

68[19]. 'Blessed be the Lord continually!
    God beareth for us the burden of our salvation.'

The costliness of salvation is recognized in the OT (see e.g. Hosea or Second Isaiah), but the full weight of the burden God bears is seen only in the Cross.

68[20b]. 'Through Yahweh, the Lord, there is deliverance from Death.'

68[25]. In the procession, the girls with the tambourines are between the singers and minstrels.

68[26]. 'In companies they greeted God,
    Even Yahweh, from Israel's spring.'

The procession has come from the spring Gihon at the foot of the temple mount (see 1 Kings 1[33-5]).

68[28-9a]. Slight changes of vowels and redivision of letters give:
    'Issue Thy commands, O my God, as befits Thy might,
    The divine might which Thou hast exercised for us.
    How potent Thou art on behalf of Jerusalem. . . .'

68[31a]. 'They are bringing bronze out of Egypt' (cf. *RSV*).

This psalm evidently belongs to the autumn festival at Jerusalem. Features found in other psalms that have been connected with that festival recur here. It would seem that after some ritual at Gihon, in which Yahweh's victory over His foes was depicted, the ark was carried in procession up to the temple as a sign that Yahweh, having chosen mount Zion for His earthly dwelling, now enters His palace as King. To this the psalm provides the choral accompaniment.

Especially noteworthy is the way ideas which have much in common with the other ancient eastern religions—the conquest of 'Death', the giving of rains, Yahweh riding on the clouds—are intertwined with themes derived from the historical traditions of Israel—the wilderness wanderings, the Sinai theophany, victories over the enemies of Israel, the Israelite confederation of tribes.

The psalm may, therefore, be set out thus:

68[1-6]. As the ark is carried forward the people raise a shout, praising Yahweh as victor over His foes. He is also celebrated as protector of the needy, orphans, widows, the lonely, and prisoners. Those who refuse to acknowledge His rule and who are not, therefore, numbered among His 'righteous' people, are condemned to the arid wastes.

68[7-14]. A reminiscence of the Song of Deborah proclaims Yahweh as the God of the wilderness wanderings, who both sends the rains and defeats His enemies in battle.

68[15-18]. The mountains of the north, sacred to the heathen gods and representing them, are jealous of Yahweh's choice of Zion as His dwelling, but He comes as a mighty victor and those who opposed Him must yield submission.

68[19-23]. Yahweh's victory brings deliverance to His people.

68[24-7]. The procession is described.

68[28-31]. The subject peoples now come to present their allegiance to Yahweh, who is urged to utter His decrees for them.

68[32-5]. The psalm ends with a triumphant hymn to Yahweh.

In spite of Paul's application of verse 18 to the risen and ascended Christ (Eph 4[8]), the vigorous expressions of this psalm are not only alien to the thought of the modern age, but seem far removed from the spirit of Jesus. Nevertheless, in a different idiom and with few inhibitions, this worship of ancient Israel proclaims convictions that are vital to any living faith. Salvation is of God, not man. He must achieve the victory, He must come and make His dwelling among men, He must rule if righteousness is to prevail. To men belong only obedience and faithfulness, acceptance of the life He makes available for them, and joyful praise of the victorious King. His is the strife and the cost, theirs the victory and the singing. Reinterpreted, this is not far from what the Christian finds in the victory of the Cross, and Paul's quotation is not merely the citing of a proof text.

69. 'Save me, O God'

One who is ill and, beset by enemies, has been deserted by his friends, utters this lament, which moves from pleading and curses to a confident hymn of praise.

69[1]. '*my soul*'. The word seems to have retained a more primitive meaning of 'neck' here (as *RSV*, cf. Jonah 2[5]). The psalmist feels that he has already sunk far into the dark waters of chaos and the underworld which represent the forces of death.

69[10a]. The meaning may be, 'I prostrated myself with fasting'.

69[21]. '*gall*'. Not merely a bitter herb, but one that is also poisonous is meant.

69[27b]. *RSV* gives the correct sense: 'may they have no acquittal from thee'.

69[28]. It was believed that those who were alive had their names on a divine 'electoral roll'. The psalmist desires the death of his enemies (cf. Ex 32[32]—where Moses shows a truly Christian attitude!—and Isa 4[3]). The verse does not carry the overtones of exclusion from everlasting life which it has for the Christian (derived from such passages as Lk 10[20], Phil 4[3], Rev 3[5]).

The urgent prayer of verses 1–21 reveals the suffering and the faith of the psalmist.

He is ill, so ill that it seems to him that the waters of death have almost overwhelmed him. Moreover, although he has made a desperate plea to God, his strength has been exhausted without receiving any answer. God appears to have deserted him (verses 1–3, 14–15).

Enemies surround him. He claims that their hatred is groundless and that their attacks show up their duplicity (verse 4). It may be that these enemies are those who accuse him of some crime—there is perhaps a hint that the charge is theft. Some have even suggested that the descriptions of his plight in verses 1–2 arise from his being imprisoned, like Jeremiah, in some dungeon (cf. Jer 38⁶), though the interpretation offered above is more likely.

If he is falsely accused, the reactions of his friends and others in the town can be readily understood. The illness is regarded as proof of guilt, for it is a divine punishment. His own family disowns the reprobate (verse 8), gossip magnifies his wickedness (verse 12), and all spurn one who is a criminal (verses 19–21). His sufferings are much like those of Job (Job 16²⁰, 17⁶⁻⁷, 19¹³⁻¹⁹, 22⁵⁻¹¹, 30¹, ⁹⁻¹⁵).

Besides the accusations of wrong doing, it seems that the psalmist is in some way persecuted for his religious zeal. His fasting and acts of self-abasement, his eagerness for the temple, and his trust in God even despite his troubles only bring insults (verses 7, 9–11).

Yet he does not despair. Repeatedly he reveals his trust in God. God knows about his sufferings and understands and cares (verse 19). He is a God whose unwavering love can be relied on, and this love is as abundant as His compassions (verses 13, 16). His help is constant and sure and He will rescue from all calamities (verse 14). If the members of his family fail in their duty of standing by a relative who is in trouble, God will act the part of kinsman and vindicate him, and he can appeal to Him with firm assurance (verse 18).

The psalmist's response to God's apparent indifference is renewed and fervent trust; his response to the attacks of his enemies is cursing. The curses of verses 22–28 have troubled many Christians, and there seems no way of mitigating them. This is what the psalmist really desired should happen to his enemies, and he believes that his curses will bring it upon them. However great the provocation, this is not the Christian way—though it may be added that many Christians have expressed very similar sentiments about their enemies in time of war with far less excuse, for Christ has died and men should have seen that the way for His followers is to 'Bless them that

persecute you; bless, and curse not' (Rom 12¹⁴), and to over-
come evil with good.

The psalm ends with a confidence which rises to a hymn of
praise (verses 30–6). Perhaps a priest has given a sign or a
prophet has spoken a word from Yahweh and the psalmist
is acquitted, but this assurance comes naturally from one who,
even when he felt far from God, could maintain his faith in
Him. God hears, God saves, God stands by His servants, and
those who seek Him have not had their faith shaken by any
unjust punishment meted out to the psalmist. These final
verses show a deep spirituality. Thanksgiving is more acceptable than unthinking offering. The blessing now enjoyed is
welcomed, not so much for the private relief it gives, as for its
confirmation of the faith of others and the revelation it contains of the merciful heart of God.

Apart from **22,** this is the psalm which NT writers quote
the most (see Mt 27³⁴, Mk 15³⁶, Jn 2¹⁷, 19²⁸⁻⁹, Acts 1²⁰,
Rom 11⁹⁻¹¹, 15³). It may have been included in some collection of testimonies to Jesus as the Messiah. But it is not
prophecy, and any reference to events in the NT is simply due
to verbal similarities or to the universal significance of suffering. Moreover, the psalmist's reaction to his afflictions was
only partially Christian. Yet if the NT conceptions of prophecy
and fulfilment are no longer tenable, they nevertheless bear
witness to the fact that the God of the OT is the Father of
Jesus Christ, and that the glimpses of His character and ways of
working which are found there come to full vision in the
incarnation.

A Note on the Curses in the Psalms

As has just been observed, the curses which are such a dis-
agreeable feature of several of the psalms must be accepted
before they can be understood. It is clear that the psalmists
fully desired the evils of which they speak to overwhelm their
enemies, as Jeremiah did (see Jer 11²⁰, 15¹⁵, 17¹⁸, 18¹⁹⁻²³).
Even if **109**⁶⁻¹⁹ is a quotation of the words of hate which the
psalmist's enemies speak against him, few of the curses in
other psalms can be eliminated in this way. Nor is it possible
to resort to allegory, and interpret the enemies as the spiritual
antagonists of the soul.

Hence our first reaction is to condemn and say, This is not

the Christian way. Indeed, it falls below other parts of the OT itself (see e.g. Gen 18$^{16-33}$, Ex 23$^{4-5}$, Lev 19^{18}, Prov 20^{22}). The days are long past when the crusader could dash out the brains of little Moslem babies with the words of 137^9 on his lips, and believe that he was serving Christ. The days should also be past when these curses could be uttered in Christian worship. It is strange that Christians should ever have thought it right to sing them, when the worst of them never had a place in the services of the synagogue.

Condemnation, however, should always be linked with an attempt to understand, and an understanding may set them in quite a new light. These psalms do not have a single background and there are a number of different factors which need to be remembered. (1) Some of the psalms which contain curses seem to be the words of those defending their innocence against criminal charges. The exaggerated language is part of the tradition of the legal setting. (2) Occasionally the psalmist may feel himself threatened by sorcerers, and he meets their enchantments with counter spells or seeks Yahweh's power to annul them. (3) Many of the curses are found in psalms spoken by those seriously ill. The mental strain of physical anguish, which was increased by the thought that the sickness was divine retribution, helps to explain these. (4) Often the enemies of the nation or the individual are regarded as the enemies of Yahweh as well. Thus they represent the forces of evil to the psalmist, rather than his purely personal enemies. (5) The effect of this last attitude is enhanced by the absence of any real hope of a future life. Evil must be defeated on the stage of this present world if right is to be triumphant. (6) Moreover, the psalmists make no distinction between the sin and the sinner as we attempt to do. Here, perhaps, it is we who are in the wrong, since sin has no existence apart from the moral agent.

Essentially, however, the curses in the psalms form part of two much wider issues: the problem of the moral consciousness of the OT, and the question of judgement. A full discussion of these points is out of the question here, but a few hints as to the lines along which a solution must be sought may be thrown out.

(*a*) *OT morality*. As William Temple emphasized, ethical decisions cannot be made in a vacuum. The distinction between right and wrong which is absolute in principle is not evident in fact. In addition, it is too readily assumed that accepted ethical standards are the immutable will of God. This is the easier because conscience presents itself to us as a categorical imperative, a demand which cannot be denied. Yet, although religion and morality have usually been closely linked, there is no immediate connexion between them, and religion is only one of the factors which mould morals. This means that morality may vary according to the historical situation, and that God may even be making different claims upon the obedience of His people according to their general spiritual condition.

To take an extreme illustration, the annihilation of Achan's whole family and all his possessions, as punishment for failing to carry out a practice repellent in itself and not even specifically Israelite (Josh 7), 'makes sense' when it is remembered that the group was the unit of reference rather than the individual in Israelite thought, and that there was an ardent desire to maintain the ethical standards of the whole nation. Even so the total destruction of Jericho was not a petty act of vengeance, but part of a holy war which Yahweh was waging against His enemies. It not only 'makes sense'; it shows that the Israelites were being utterly loyal to Yahweh *in that particular situation*. If they had not acted in that way then, they might never have risen beyond those conceptions. Thus the psalms which now give offence to us may represent a proper response to the righteous will of Yahweh.

But if this approach is correct, it presents a terrifying doubt to the Christian mind of today, as well as offering a word of comfort. The doubt arises from the fact that we too are children of our age, and our consciences are imperfect and conditioned by the society in which we have been brought up. To us Pascal's aphorism becomes an ugly threat: 'Men never do evil so fully and so happily as when they do it for conscience sake'. The comfort lies in God's acceptance of the response we make to the moral demand, if honestly given after deliberate thought. After all, the only possible way to act is that which a friar urges in one of Housman's plays: 'Do always what you believe right, brother; and if that is wrong, repent of it afterwards'.

(b) *Judgement*. Modern sentimentalism, coupled with the making of a violent and false contrast between the two testaments and between 'law' and 'grace', has led to the virtual elimination of judgement from Christian thought today. Yet judgement (and hell) is clearly set out in the teaching of Jesus (see Mt 11$^{21-4}$, 13$^{24-30}$, 23$^{13-39}$, 25$^{31-46}$, Mk 9$^{42-8}$, 12$^{1-9}$, 14^{21}). If we take Christ seriously, we must take judgement seriously as well. We have no right to pick out only such parts of His teaching as are agreeable to the spirit of the age.

A large part of our difficulties over judgement arises from three misconceptions. (1) We imagine that punishment is a deliberately inflicted pain which is completely unconnected with the wrong done. This may be true of the punishments which men inflict upon others; it is not true of the divine judgements. (2) We often fail to see that whether suffering is regarded as punishment depends entirely upon the attitude of the sinner. All punishment is merely vindictive to the man who will not recognize his guilt, but the penitent welcomes the punishment as a means of cleansing his stain. (3) We tend to value material wealth and earthly happiness above moral goodness and spiritual riches, and as a consequence will not believe that the punishment of the sin is often to have obtained the sinful thing which we desired (see Mt 6^2, Lk 6^{24}, 16^{25}).

Once it is grasped, however, that man's highest good is the enjoyment of God as He really is, that God and evil are more opposed than yes and no, than black and white, and that sin only has meaning in terms of the sinner, judgement falls into place. The self-centred soul which sees God and turns away in hatred and horror, deliberately choosing evil rather than good, can only come to judgement. To go to heaven would be hell for such a man. As Dante saw so clearly when he wrote above the gate of hell, 'Divine Power, Supreme Wisdom, Primal Love made me', God's love makes hell by merely existing. Humanity's tragedy is that sin is both attractive—else no one would ever follow it—and destructive of all man's good.

From this it follows that: (1) earthly loss *may* be a means to a man's salvation. It is not impossible, therefore, to pray for the downfall of evil men, not only for the sake of those whom they are injuring, but also for their own sake, since to go on and on in sin and get away with it may be the ultimate hurt. (2) The Christian must acquiesce in God's judgement, for not to do so is to have failed to choose whole-heartedly for God. Tolerance is not kindliness, but a failure to recognize sin for what it is and to reject it.

Yet even so we may well shrink from seeking judgement on others. We too are sinners, uncertain of God's will and continually failing to perform it. Rationalizing is all too easy. Faults are most glaringly apparent in our personal enemies. Even with men whose wickedness is blatant and clear, we are ignorant of the circumstances which made them what they are and of the hidden motives by which they act. Nor must we think that as a man is so he will ever remain—it is only at the gates of hell that the inscription reads, 'Abandon hope, all ye that enter here'. And our hesitation has the support of Christ, who spoke stern words about judging others, and who always sides with those whom others condemned (see Mt 7¹⁻⁵, Mk 2¹⁸⁻²⁰, ²³⁻⁸, 7⁵⁻¹⁵, 9³⁸⁻⁴⁰, 14³⁻⁹, Lk 7³⁶⁻⁵⁰, 9⁵¹⁻⁶).

70. 'Do not tarry, O my God'

See on 40¹³⁻¹⁷.

71. Prayer Grounded in Experience and Hastening to Praise

An old man (verses 9, 17–18), who has been overtaken by some trouble, probably sickness, and who suffers from the hostility of enemies, prays to Yahweh for deliverance. No clear outline of the psalm can be discerned; petition, confident trust, imprecation, vows, and joyful praise jostle each other in eager prayer. There are reminiscences of several other psalms (e.g. verses 1–3, cf. 31¹⁻³), but these seem to be less direct quotation than the mark of a devotion that has been nourished by earlier psalms and naturally expresses itself in well loved phrases.

71³. *RSV*, adopting a small change, is better:

> 'Be thou to me a rock of refuge,
>   a strong fortress, to save me,
>   for thou art my rock and my fortress.'

71⁷. *'a wonder'*. The psalmist means that he is regarded as a typical example of divine punishment (cf. verse 11).

In an age when God was regarded, not as an absentee Deity about whom some facts may be believed, but as an active

Participant in the affairs of men, misfortune was all too easily considered a sign of divine wrath. This appears to have happened to the psalmist. Despite a life-time of faithfulness to God, sickness which has brought him near to death has come upon him (verse 20), and his enemies draw their cruel conclusions (verses 4, 7, 10–11). In his distress he makes his appeal to God.

His prayer is urgent (cf. verses 1–3, 12); yet this psalm stands out among other similar laments for the confident trust which the psalmist reveals. He delights in repeating words which speak of the security there is in Yahweh. He is Refuge, Rock and Fortress, the sure hope of those who trust in Him and the One upon whose faithfulness ('*truth*') men can rely. The psalmist also recalls that Yahweh is a God who acts decisively to save His servants (this is the significance of '*righteousness*' in verses 2, 15 and 24). This is no dead creed, dully repeated. It is a faith which, nourished by experience, is firm and living (see verses 5–6, 17).

Like the writer of **69,** this psalmist desires the downfall of his enemies, but he shows none of the vehemence of those cursings. A brief glance at their discomfiture and then a return to God's deliverance is his way. He has so much to tell of God's goodness, and he makes such ardent vows to give Him thankful praise, that he has no time to gloat over their misery. Condemnation is a young man's fault, and some would see in this more mellow attitude a mark of the psalmist's age. It is, perhaps, experience alone which can teach that invective seldom produces amendment, and too easily damages the spirit of the one who utters his denunciation.

The confident trust which appears throughout the psalm springs into a blaze at the end. God has watched over him even from the time before he was born. This God cannot now abandon him. Soon he will be able once again to sing His praises and teach others of His mighty salvation (verses 14–18, 21–4).

72. The righteous King

This royal psalm, a prayer that the king may faithfully fulfil his high office, and that, since righteousness is the foundation of prosperity, his reign may promote the true welfare of his people, seems to have been sung at the accession of the king in Jerusalem. The verbs should be read as petitions (as *RSV*).

72³, ⁷. *'peace'*, i.e. 'welfare'—see on **29**.

72⁵ᵃ. This seems out of place, whether the object is regarded as the king or Yahweh. It is best to follow the Greek version and read, 'May he continue' (cf. *RSV*).

72⁸. *'the River'*. This may be the Euphrates, but it has been suggested that it is the cosmic sea which was regarded as providing the life of the holy city (cf. **46⁴**). On either interpretation a world-wide kingdom is intended.

72¹⁵. *'they shall live'*. The Hebrew has 'he'. This is a wish for the king—'may he flourish'.

72¹⁶. *'shall shake'*. The verb may mean, 'may (it) be plenteous'.

72¹⁸⁻¹⁹. This is probably the doxology at the end of the second book of the Psalter. It is not to be despised on that account. Jewish liturgy fills out the note of joyous praise of God which is sometimes lacking in Christian devotion, and this doxology is a fine expression of such adoration.

Opening with a prayer that the king may rule his people in righteousness, and that he may thus prosper himself and also be a blessing to his people (verses 1–7), the psalmist looks for an enlargement of the king's sovereignty until the whole world is subjected to him (verses 8–11). This is not a lust for political power devoid of spiritual and religious feelings. It is granted to the king only as he rules his people justly, and the next section explores the meaning of this royal justice (verses 12–14). The final verses return to the thought of prosperity for the king and his nation.

The psalm is not only important for the vivid picture it presents of the place of the king in the life of ancient Israel, but also for the insight into the ethical thought of the OT which it gives.

The foundation belief is that Yahweh is actively concerned with the life of Israel. He is the source of both moral righteousness and material prosperity. From this two convictions emerge.

(1) The welfare of the nation depends on the morality which

is practised within it. Only if men's lives are governed by right principles will they prosper. In the psalm this is worked out in ways that are somewhat foreign to us. The primary need in the ancient world was for fruitfulness in field and home, and thus prosperity is primarily depicted as abundance of crops. Moreover, the king, as ruler and representative of his people, has a decisive part to play in their welfare. Only if his character is upright and his government exhibits righteousness will his people be able to live out the good life.

(2) Righteousness is no man-made scale of values, but comes from God Himself. His will is the standard by which king and people must act. Thus the specific justice which is laid upon the king is to give special protection to those in danger of being oppressed and downtrodden. This care of the under-privileged is a mark of the OT righteousness, as can be seen in Jeremiah's comment upon king Josiah (Jer 22[15-16]), or in Isaiah's condemnation of those who wrong the orphan and the widow who have none to defend them (Isa 1[23]), and springs from the conviction that Yahweh's way was ever to defend the helpless and care for the poor. Moreover, because the king's justice is derived from Yahweh, he is both dependent on Him and responsible to Him for his conduct of the nation's affairs.

These ideas will need to be formulated afresh for the world of today; yet it can hardly be doubted that as principles they still stand. Few would deny that it is an intangible spiritual power which makes a nation great, and that the quest for false ends together with a lowered regard for moral values breeds that instability which issues in anti-social behaviour and a purposelessness that imperils industrial relations. The importance of the lead which a government can give is also apparent. Even in a democracy, a responsible government should be ahead of popular opinion, and in the interaction of law and custom should aim at raising the levels of behaviour in society, instead of being too ready to sacrifice righteousness to popularity.

The second principle can also be reasserted. In an age when morality is increasingly being regarded as relative and when ethics and the individual conscience are said to be entirely the result of social pressures, the divine basis of an absolute ethic is in danger of being dismissed. Social and psychological laws impose limitations, but they do not dispose of the righteousness

that comes from God. And on a less theoretical level, the
Christian ethic proclaims with even greater force than the OT
that it is not the privileged but the deprived who must be
given the greater help.

In Jewish and Christian tradition, though not in the NT
itself, this psalm has been regarded as messianic prophecy; the
Aramaic paraphrase renders verse 1 as,

> 'O God, give the precepts of Thy judgement to King Messiah
> And Thy righteousness to the son of king David',

while in the Early Church it was sung at the Epiphany. This
was not the original intention of the psalmist, but the Christian
will have no hesitation in saying that only in Christ Jesus
is there a king whose character and rule are perfectly righteous,
and who can therefore be granted that universal sovereignty
where every knee bows to Him and all men call Him Lord.